IT GETS
TO BE
EASY
(IF YOU LET IT)

THE ART OF AUTHENTICITY AND OTHER LIFE LESSONS WE SKIPPED

BY JULIA HENNING, PSY.M.

IT GETS TO BE EASY (IF YOU LET IT)

THE ART OF AUTHENTICITY AND OTHER LIFE LESSONS WE SKIPPED

JULIA HENNING

To anyone and everyone who has forgotten
that life gets to be easy,
and to Jooj, who finally remembered

HEY THERE, DEAR READERS!

Before we dive into the main course of this book, here's a little something extra to sweeten the deal. Throughout these pages, you'll find a whisk icon (this book is heavy on cooking metaphors.) Each whisk leads to a resource that goes hand in hand with that section of the book. When you see a whisk, that's your cue to scan the QR code that will take you to a private online page of bonus goodies!

Think downloadable worksheets, interactive audio, and mastermind programs that pair perfectly with everything you'll be cooking up in these chapters.

→ **Free Samples:** Grab some tasty, free downloads to keep you simmering with inspiration! Here, you'll find fill-in-the-blank activities, breakdowns of techniques, and in-depth prompts for deeper reflection. You'll see the title of each resource paired with the section title in the book. Plus, you'll get an extended resource list of all references and sources in the book!

→ **Gourmet Programs:** Ready for a feast? My paid *It Gets to Be Easy* Mastermind and 22-Day Cosmic Concoction Manifestation Challenge are the gourmet meals of personal growth. *And?* To receive the ultimate *It Gets to Be Easy* "Recipe for Success" discount on these premium programs, use the code **"ease"** at checkout!

Scan the QR code to unlock a pantry full of delicious extras!

INTRODUCTION

Have you ever stood at the edge of a precipice, gazing out at the expansive horizon, feeling the gentle breeze tousling your hair and the warm sun painting the sky in hues of orange and pink? In that moment, did a sense of peace wash over you, momentarily quieting the incessant demands of emails and text messages, easing the existential fear that you might be missing your life's purpose?

Oscar Wilde once quipped something to the effect that life is too important to be taken seriously. Perhaps your initial reaction to this idea is skepticism, as if the visualization above and the use of this quote were plucked from a carefully curated Pinterest board. After all, don't success and fulfillment require relentless pursuit, a perpetual climb up an unforgiving mountain? Isn't life a series of challenges, battles, and hard-won victories requiring sweat, tears, and blood (usually once a month for three to seven days, give or take, with cramps and bloating)?

But what if Wilde was onto something? What if life could be easier, more joyful, and less about the struggle? What if the key to happiness and fulfillment isn't constantly striving but rather finding ease amid the chaos? Consider this: What if there's a way to live where you're not continually pushing a boulder uphill, only to watch it roll back down and crush your spirit? What if there's a path that allows you to achieve without sacrificing your sanity, where success flows naturally from a place of authenticity and alignment?

Everyone tells you to just be yourself, but no one really teaches you *how* to be yourself. In fact, most of the world doesn't *want* you to be yourself. In a society that capitalizes on your self-doubt, liking and knowing yourself is a radical act (more on that later). And this is where the art of authenticity comes in—a concept that, frankly, should have been a class in school but got left out of the curriculum, along with how to do taxes and why you shouldn't put aluminum foil in the microwave. I believe this book contains some crucial life lessons—lessons I wish we were all taught early on, and ones I hope to introduce you to in a way that makes them stick.

I've been there, navigating the complexities of life and discovering that it gets to be easy if you let it. This book is not just a collection of insights; it's a guide to embracing simplicity and finding joy in the process of reclaiming your sense of peace amid life's demands.

Welcome to *It Gets to Be Easy (If You Let It): The Art of Authenticity and Other Life Lessons We Skipped*, a manual for unlocking a life filled with purpose, authenticity, and yes, ease—complete with twists, turns, and occasional overshares. This book is your guide to transforming your mindset, embracing ease, and creating a life of acceptance where your special sauce is your secret weapon. (Wait until chapter 8!) It's not about finding shortcuts or dodging responsibilities; it's about aligning your actions with your deeper desires and allowing life to unfold naturally.

I'll get to the complete introduction in a minute, but before we go any further, I'm Julia, the mind behind these words and the voice in your head after finishing the book. (Sorry, not sorry!) You see, for the longest time, I believed that to succeed, I had to hustle harder than everyone else. I was the queen of burnout, the champion of overcommitment, and the patron saint of stressing out over every little detail. Sound familiar?

I subscribed to the belief that success hinged on outward achievements and societal validation. Then, through the subtle guidance of the universe (going beyond horoscopes), the gradual embrace of authenticity (years of therapy), and an unwavering commitment to personal integrity (putting my money where my mouth is), I discovered the true essence of a life filled with ease. This realization reshaped my entire life.

Let me take you back to the beginning, which, in this case, was in the depths of the Costa Rican jungle. Now, picture this: I'm surrounded by the thick, humid air of the rainforest, sitting in a circle of twenty-two women I had just met, preparing to drink ayahuasca for the first time, and it's only night one...of four. The atmosphere is electric with anticipation, the sounds of the jungle buzzing around us. As the ceremony begins and the brew takes effect, I'm plunged into a realm of profound introspection (and the vision of a panther staring at me from across the room, but that's another story).

In this altered state, ayahuasca spoke to me. It wasn't a whisper but a powerful, clear message: "You will write a book." The title was given to me as if it had always been a part of my soul—*It Gets to Be Easy (If You Let It)*. At first, it seemed like a riddle, a piece of wisdom wrapped in mystery.

I wish I could say I went home the next day and started typing away, but life is rarely that straightforward. It took me over a year, countless false starts, and a ton of personal growth to finally connect the dots, unravel what this book was meant to be, and embrace the ease it promised. I had to learn the hard way—through trial and error, and a lot of soul-searching—how to actually let life be easy.

So, who am I to dish out my thoughts on this topic? I'm Julia Henning, a certified life coach with a master's in psychology. I've spent over a decade facilitating mindfulness groups and individual sessions, started two successful companies before turning thirty, and created critically acclaimed theatrical productions and live events. I am a voice-over artist and host a highly rated podcast called *The Permission Portal*, with another on the way. (It's called *Not Another Self-Help Podcast*; we figured we'd be upfront about it.) Beyond this, I'm a food-loving, dance-like-no-one's-watching, idea-loving wild child at heart (who will forever wear sneakers over high heels to any formal event).

Résumé aside, I'm just a "regular gal" (hormones, anxiety, and expectations included) who's been through the trenches and lived to tell the tale. I've started over countless times, failed or quit more times than that, and even survived a few emotional breakdowns along the way. With all this living, I still found myself questioning if I was doing enough, being enough. But through it all, I've learned one valuable lesson: life doesn't have to be a never-ending struggle. My journey has been one of relentless pursuit but also one of profound transformation. I talk about being human for a living (yes, people pay me for this). For me, getting to revel in the human experience is a life of ease, but it took a long time for it to feel easy.

In today's fast-paced world, it's easy to lose sight of what truly matters amid the noise of external expectations and societal pressures. We often find ourselves chasing after external validation, material possessions, or fleeting moments of happiness, only to realize that true fulfillment comes from within.

This book isn't about shortcuts or bypassing effort. It's about redefining your relationship with expectations, success, and fulfillment. It's about recognizing that ease doesn't mean a lack of action but rather a harmonious alignment of your actions with your true self. In this book, we're gonna dive deep into the art of making life easier. Oscar Wilde's idea about life being too important to be taken seriously champions this very approach. It's not about trivializing life but understanding that the gravity of life's importance doesn't have to equate to constant struggle and seriousness.

Through the pages of this book, my goal is to equip you with practical strategies to make mindful life moves, embrace your authenticity, and let go of the belief that the life your heart desires is made only of sacrifices and compromises. You will learn to cultivate self-awareness, embrace your strengths, overcome your limitations, and unleash your inner dragon (power, I mean power!).

But remember, the title is *It Gets to Be Easy (If You Let It)*; true transformation requires courage, commitment, and action. As you delve into the pages ahead, I encourage you to embrace the discomfort of growth and approach this journey with an open mind and a willingness to challenge yourself—and to change.

Ultimately, *It Gets to Be Easy (If You Let It)* is not just a book—it's a call to action. It's an invitation, or even a permission slip, to take over the driver's seat of your life and remember who the f— you are (not who you think you should be). From that place, you can live your life as it was meant to be lived, as peacefully as possible (despite gravity, natural disasters, technology—you get the point). So, are you ready to let it be easy and create a life you love? If so, then turn the dang page already! But let's make one thing clear if I haven't yet: the path to ease is not always easy.

PART 1

EASE UP

Understand ease and what gets in
the way of it.

CHAPTER 1

EASE ISN'T EASY

"If you're not doing what you love, you're wasting your time."

—Billy Joel

SHATTERING THE ILLUSION

So, I *was* going to start this chapter with a song lyric, but copyright infringement is a real thing—and I'd rather not get sued by a certain piano man who's got a lot to say about passion, pride, and the foolishness of chasing satisfaction (*hint:* head to Vienna).

But even without the direct lyrics, his other statement gets to the point. I love starting chapters with the right words because they set the tone...with ease. Finding the expression that best depicts decades of life lived to start a paragraph is overwhelming. It's a challenge, battling the desire to achieve perfection in a handful of pages. It's tough taking the first steps and writing the first words. Using a quote is like having a seasoned guide who's already trekked the path we're about to explore. And frankly, figuring out how to start a chapter can be as daunting as deciding on the perfect playlist for a road trip. You want it to flow, captivate, and make sense of everything that comes after.

Okay, I'll admit it wasn't a poolside vacay sourcing these quotes and unwrapping their meanings. You'll learn that I, in fact, tend to make things more challenging for myself in an effort to create ease for others. I utilize my experience as a source of integrated wisdom for those seeking support. (I'm a life coach writing a book about ease, remember?) But here we are, at the start of our first chapter and our first nugget of ease. You may also notice my choice to refrain from using the word "lesson," as my intention with this book is to offer you the opportunity for perspective, not tell you what to do.

There is a reason I reveal my quote process to you up front. Deciding how to captivate you from the start can be daunting. So why not borrow a bit of wisdom from someone who's already nailed it? Your first nugget of ease: don't reinvent the wheel when you don't have to. Being human is already hard enough, but more on that later.

No matter who you are, where you come from, or what you do, being human is like being handed a recipe with half the instructions missing. You've got to figure out the rest on your own, and sometimes, it feels like you're just making a mess in the kitchen. But those missing instructions? The gaps are not a mistake. They're the secret ingredients that force you to improvise, adapt, and thrive.

Billy Joel's lyrics perfectly capture this paradox. You might have your passion and pride, but if you think satisfaction comes easily, you're fooling yourself. True ease isn't about avoiding challenges. It's about developing a resilient mindset that gracefully helps you navigate them. Think of it like cooking a gourmet meal. You might have the finest ingredients—your passion and pride— but without the proper techniques and the willingness to tackle a few culinary disasters, you won't create anything extraordinary. Those burnt edges and failed attempts? They're teaching moments, pushing you to become a better chef. Similarly, life's obstacles are not just hurdles but opportunities for growth. They force us to adapt, innovate, and ultimately, thrive.

The allure of "easy" is strong. It's tempting to believe that if things come easily, we'll be satisfied. We yearn for simplicity, for things to fall into place without much effort. But this is where the deception of "easy" comes into play. Satisfaction that comes too easily can be shallow and fleeting. It's like opting for fast food over a home-cooked meal—sure, it fills you up quickly, but it doesn't nourish you in the same way. Letting life be easy means embracing a mindset that welcomes growth and learning from those challenges. It's about finding peace and contentment in the process, not just achieving certain outcomes.

When we focus on ease, we engage fully with what makes us tick, taking pride in our efforts and understanding that the journey is where the magic happens. It's about developing the resilience to bounce back from setbacks, staying present in the moment, and accepting things as they are (and as we are).

So, let's dive into a life of ease, where true fulfillment isn't a far-off dream but a daily practice. How might we embrace the beautifully messy, wonderfully challenging path to real ease?

Simple! We shatter the illusion of *easy*.

EASY VS. EASE

"Easy" implies avoiding challenges, taking the path of least resistance, and seeking comfort. Think of those moments when you've chosen the easy route—skipping your workout for a binge-watching session, avoiding a tough conversation because it felt awkward. Sure, it feels good in the moment, but over time, it can lead to stagnation and missed opportunities. Easy is all about short-term satisfaction. You just don't *feel as good*. Easy has a habit of focusing on an outcome.

By contrast, *ease* is the quality of being at peace in your circumstances and feeling confident in your own skin. True ease comes from within and is cultivated through awareness, resilience, acceptance, and mindful practice. It's not about avoiding the gym but finding joy in the process of staying fit. It's not about dodging tough conversations but approaching them with clarity and faith. Ease is about long-term fulfillment and well-being. Ease favors the process. It's good to feel good.

So, why did I call this book *It Gets to Be Easy (If You Let It)*? Why use the word "easy" instead of "ease"? Let's own our shit for a second: "Easy" is what we're all secretly craving, isn't it? We want life to feel simple, smooth, and unburdened by constant struggle. Sure, we may crave some discipline or get off on unlocking new levels through hard work. But ultimately, after a long day of navigating the path toward fulfillment and even basic survival, do we as a species yearn for that process to be *more complicated*? Despite different practices and ideologies, beneath almost every belief system lies the idea that the path to making life feel easy is cultivating ease. It's about doing the inner work, building resilience, and embracing authenticity.

When I say it gets to be easy if you let it, I'm highlighting the paradox that true ease in life doesn't come from avoiding challenges but from changing our mindset toward them. You'll see this phrase woven throughout the book, not because I missed it during editing, but because it's a reminder we often dismiss. Most of us have been taught, consciously or not, to brush off advice like this, assuming it's just a cliché. But here, it's essential. **Life Lesson:** Changing your mindset isn't a one-time tip; it's the foundation for creating a life where ease feels real and possible. It's about allowing ourselves to navigate through hardships with grace and composure, transforming our internal landscape so that external challenges don't derail us. The goal is to make life easy by choosing a path of ease and developing the tools and mindset that make handling life's detours more manageable. We're not aiming to dodge every curveball life throws at us. Instead, we're learning to catch them with poise and maybe even a little style.

Alright, it's time for a visual! Imagine you're at a gathering with friends. You have two choices of drinks: a glass of wine or a shot of tequila. The wine is smooth, familiar, and easy to sip. It's comfortable and relaxing, a go-to option when you want to unwind without much effort. The tequila shot, on the other hand, is bold and intense. It might burn a bit going down, but it can lead to a night of laughter, dancing, and unforgettable memories.

For those seeking a more natural libation, let's imagine the choice between a soothing cup of herbal tea or a zesty ginger shot. The tea is warm, comforting, and easy to enjoy. It's your reliable friend for a quiet evening. The ginger shot, however, is fiery and invigorating. It wakes your senses and gives you a burst of energy, setting the stage for a day of adventurous choices (and—bonus!—a regulated digestive system).

So, let's break down the difference between "easy" and "ease" with these metaphors. "Easy" is like that glass of wine or cup of tea. It's familiar, it's simple, and it doesn't push you out of your comfort zone. But if you only stick to what's easy, you might miss out on the vibrant, unpredictable experiences life offers.

"Ease," on the other hand, is like taking that tequila or ginger shot. It requires a bit more courage and can be a little uncomfortable at first, but it's about embracing the unexpected, finding joy in new experiences, and knowing that while not every moment will be smooth, each one will be rich with potential.

EMBRACING EASE

So, here's my apology if you were expecting a life hack that's as simple and straightforward as sipping a glass of wine or tea. This journey we're on together? It's going to have its tequila or ginger shot moments—intense, challenging, but ultimately rewarding. Embracing ease means leaning into these moments, savoring the richness they bring, and coming out stronger and more fulfilled on the other side. Cheers to the adventure!

A life without challenges seems like the golden ticket after a long day of hustling to survive. It sounds easier, right? If we had all the answers to life's questions handed to us, we wouldn't have to try so hard. Everything we desired would manifest with just a thought. We'd be happier, right? (Don't come for me, Law of Attraction devotees; we all know it takes a bit more than just positive thinking.)

But if you knew how to win the game up front, would you even play? A life that seems easy can lead to complacency and a lack of progress. You know the saying that "the grass is always greener"? People who avoid challenges tend to miss out on personal growth and fulfillment. We always want what we don't have.

Consider your own life for a moment. Think back to the tougher eras. In fact, think back to the most challenging time you've ever faced. Maybe it was a heartbreak, a job loss, a health scare, or just a period of feeling lost and directionless. Those times probably felt like being trapped in a snow globe, shaken by some amused kid while you were stuck in the middle as the elements of your life chaotically swirled around you.

There's this common belief, especially in Western cultures, that equates suffering with growth. It's as if our collective consciousness decided that if we're not struggling, we're not moving forward. *If it doesn't burn, it ain't workin'!* But here's a thought: how you view these challenges changes how you respond to them. If you see them as insurmountable obstacles, that's what they'll be. But if you see them as opportunities for growth, they suddenly become a lot less intimidating. Looking back, can you see how they shaped you into who you are today? How they forced you to dig deep, find your strength, and grow in ways you never thought possible? As my Gen Z assistant would enthusiastically clap at me and say, *"PERIOD!"*

BALANCING EASE

So, what's the secret sauce? True ease isn't about dodging hardships. It's about building the resilience and mindset to navigate them effectively. It's choosing what you suffer over. Choosing which challenges to take on. Picking your battles.

The reticular activating system (RAS) in your brain mediates your behavior and perception. True ease isn't about avoiding hardships; it's about building resilience and focusing on what truly matters. The RAS acts like a bouncer, filtering out distractions—like irrelevant worries, unproductive tasks, or toxic influences—so that you can focus on meaningful opportunities that align with your goals. By consciously choosing to see challenges as growth opportunities, your RAS amplifies this focus, making it easier to identify and act on the things that genuinely propel you forward. Now, you're focused on the VIPs in your life that deserve your attention. This perspective reinforces the idea that things happen *for* you, not *to* you.

If life were easy, what would be the point of survival?

Life Lesson: Balancing ambition with ease is the name of the game. Take a look at those who nail this balance without burning out. Successful individuals embody ease without sacrificing ambition. They set goals that stretch them but keep their well-being front and center. They understand that true success isn't just about achievement but also about how you feel along the way.

When discussing this topic with one of my coaching clients, I asked her to identify an individual who embodies ease. Without hesitation, she said Taylor Swift. As a low-key Swiftie, I was shocked I hadn't thought of Swift myself. And yes, I am about to make an example out of her sincerely. Taylor Swift has a song in which she claims she "can do it with a broken heart." Despite the unfathomable ride of being the most famous person in the world, Taylor Swift embodies ease by being herself in everything she offers us, cringe and all. She owns her cringe. She performs when it's tough. She bares her soul to the world in an effort to create peace and solace for others (sound familiar?). Taylor often reminds us she wouldn't want to be doing anything else, nor should we expect her to be. It doesn't mean it's easy, but for her, it's authentic. For Taylor Swift, unbridled fame and recognition is ease.

ACTING INTO AUTHENTICITY

Let's talk about my adolescent flirtation with acting. Yep, I ~~was~~ am a theater kid. I grew up idolizing my older siblings, who introduced me to the world of performing as an after-school hobby. While they chose more practical paths, I earnestly pursued acting as a career. For me, getting on stage and performing a monologue felt easy. And, being totally candid here, having a natural inclination for the art didn't hurt. (Who am I kidding? I'm a talented actress.)

When it was time to choose a path to self-sufficiency, everyone around me seemed to pick skills or careers that guaranteed a linear progression toward success— stability, societal acceptance, and a proven method to achieve material comfort. But not me. I chose what felt easy. Acting is challenging, but I thought becoming a professional actress was my meal ticket to an easy life of reward and praise. To get my degree, I rolled around on the floor, painted my face like a cat, and spoke in accents, all while dreaming of a life of splendor and fame. Life was going to be easy, I thought. I wasn't going to work as hard as the finance kids or the communication majors!

But when I moved to Hollywood, the ease I thought I had secured for myself quickly faded. The illusion shattered. I felt a bitter pill get stuck in my throat and stay there for years—I realized that in choosing something that appeared easy, I hadn't prepared myself for a life of authentic ease. I couldn't see the bigger picture of the challenges I would face by resting on my laurels (even if those laurels could speak in five distinguished British accents). For me, easy meant landing roles in smaller productions where I could be the big fish in a small pond rather than taking the leap to the main stages. I would choose monologues that spoke to my life experiences instead of challenging myself with denser material.

I didn't realize any of this until I tried to play the Hollywood game. Nothing is easy in Hollywood except for the decision to go there. After years of mild achievements and a few quarter-life crises, I began to doubt myself. I wasn't landing roles I thought were made for me. I wasn't making the kind of money needed to survive. I couldn't offer anything impressive when everyone asked me, "Have you been in anything I've seen?"

It took a harrowing disagreement with a director during the rehearsal of a Shakespeare play for me to truly grasp the difference between ease and easy. To others, it might have seemed like a small issue, a typical clash in the world of theater: after confronting another actor for not taking the process seriously and making personal remarks about their performance, the director turned the tables and asked me to perform the very section he had criticized—right in front of the entire cast. I found myself in an uncomfortable position.

For many actors, this moment could have felt like an opportunity—a chance to step into the spotlight and prove themselves. But for me, it felt wrong. I could have complied, swallowed my discomfort, and done what he asked. That would have been the "easy" thing to do. But my gut screamed at me: *No!* The director hadn't just called me to perform; he had publicly humiliated my fellow actor, and then he expected me to participate in that same cruelty. This wasn't the usual director's authority—it was something that cut deeper, something that made me feel unsafe and exposed. So I said no.

He pushed back, insisting that the show must go on and that I either perform or leave. So I left—not just the rehearsal, but the entire pursuit of a professional acting career.

Some might say I took the easy way out by quitting. But in reality, that decision came from a place of deep alignment with my values. The "easy" path actually would have been to stay, keep my head down, and play along. But there was no *ease* left in that situation. Ease, to me, is about being in flow, in harmony with yourself and your surroundings. It's when your actions reflect your inner truth. In that moment, staying would have felt like betraying myself. True ease came from walking away and honoring who I was and what I stood for. What looked easy to others—staying in the game, following orders—would have been suffocating to me. True ease didn't lie in compliance; it lay in the courage to say no, to step away, and to trust that there was a path more aligned with my values waiting for me.

That's the trickiness of "easy." Quitting acting felt like an escape from immediate stress and conflict, which might look like "the easy way out." However, this decision wasn't about avoiding challenges; it was about recognizing when something no longer aligned with my true path. By refusing to comply and walking away, I chose a different kind of ease—the kind that aligned with my true self rather than what others demanded of me. This decision wasn't about avoiding effort; it was about refusing to compromise my integrity and values. Instead, I chose to embrace the path that felt right deep down in my soul. This kind of ease, the one that aligns with who you truly are, is what we're after. If you and your soul are not on the same page, expect the pages of this book to help with that.

Walking away from everything I'd built—my efforts, achievements, reputation, community—wasn't easy. The only easy part was realizing that the life I had constructed didn't bring me true ease and didn't honor who I felt I was deep down. Entertaining an audience had been easy, but genuine human connection and service are where I find my true ease. I wanted to help people by being myself, sharing my stories, and creating meaningful interactions that could inspire change. I no longer felt at ease playing a character, reciting lines someone else had written, and delivering a rehearsed outcome. This realization led to my life-changing decision.

Now, I'm not a big believer in labels, because we're all so much more than what we do. But for the sake of the story, I decided to trade in my acting career to live as a healer—a self-help facilitator, a counselor, and an entrepreneur in the business of human connection and the human condition. This decision took me to grad school to get my master's in psychology (more on that pivotal moment in chapter 2!). It was one of the biggest decisions I had ever made—to embark on a new path and change my life, and to devote myself to more work than I had ever done before. It required more discipline and sacrifice than I had ever faced. But for the first time, it wasn't comfort driving me; it was a deeper sense of ease, authenticity, and alignment. The outcome was uncertain, but the process felt right. I felt right. So, I took the proverbial tequila shot and let inspiration guide me. This is ease: allowing inspiration to guide your actions and embracing authenticity as your compass.

THE EASE ESSENTIALS

Alright, now that we've tackled the difference between ease and easy, let's get cozy and explore the essentials that will guide us on this journey toward a life that feels good— like, genuinely good. Think of this book as a cookbook of life lessons, whipping up a delightful dish of fulfillment and ease. Before we dive into the hand-crafted recipes (aka chapters), consider the following to be the staple ingredients in the pantry of ease. Yes, I love my analogies, and again, I'm not sorry for it!

Here are the ease essentials:

→ **Inner peace** means maintaining a calm and centered mind regardless of external chaos. It's about finding contentment within yourself without needing outside validation, and being okay with who you are and where you are, even when things aren't perfect.

→ **Resilience** comes from developing the ability to bounce back from setbacks, which builds mental and emotional strength. Resilience isn't about never falling; it's about rising every time you do. It's seeing challenges as opportunities for growth rather than insurmountable obstacles. Like Taylor Swift, we learn to "shake it off" and keep going.

→ **Mindfulness and presence** allow you to be fully present and savor the moment. They keep you grounded and reduce anxiety about the future. Use these essentials to enjoy the little things and not let your mind wander too far ahead.

→ **Acceptance** looks like embracing things as they are rather than fighting to change them. This doesn't mean giving up but rather focusing on what you can control—like Taylor owning her "cringe" moments and turning them into art. (Oh yeah, I'm sticking with TSwift on this one; can we deny her success rate?!)

→ **Aligned action** means taking steps that align with your values and true self. This ensures your efforts lead to genuine fulfillment. Pursue goals with intention and authenticity, not out of obligation or societal pressure. It's about doing what you say you are going to do. Taylor wanted world domination, and with every album, easter egg, and lyric she offered, she got it. (If you have no idea what I am talking about, it's okay; just go with it or Google the girl.)

→ **Balanced living** results from striking a balance between effort and relaxation, work and play, ambition and contentment. Prioritizing well-being alongside productivity leads to a harmonious life. It's about mixing the perfect cocktail of hustle and chill.

Maybe you're thinking, *Okay, okay, I get it! Ease isn't easy! Let's do something about it then!* Don't worry! As I said before, this book will arm you with practical strategies to support you in finding your ease. I'll now offer you the first step in crafting the life you deeply desire. Mark the journey and decide how you want to feel every day. Start with a Passion Pledge.

YOUR PASSION PLEDGE

STEP 1: UNLEASH YOUR DEEPER DESIRE

What do you want?

To craft your Passion Pledge, you must become aware of what you are pledging to do. Download the Passion Pledge worksheet, or on a separate sheet, I invite you to begin with some reflective journaling.

First, take a few moments to clear your mind and get comfortable. Ask yourself: What do you deeply desire? No shame, no guilt, no doubt. What do you truly want out of life? Write down whatever comes to mind. Don't overthink it; let your thoughts flow freely.

Journal Prompt:

My desire is _____.

Consider the following examples:

→ My desire is a job that offers me more money.

→ My desire is a relationship that provides more fulfillment and connection.

→ My desire is to discover hobbies or skills that bring me more joy and confidence.

→ My desire is to wake up every day with ease.

I'll go a step further and offer you my desire in writing this book: *My desire is to write a book I am proud to publish and share.* It is simple, truthful, and tangible.

Your reflection might mirror the examples provided, or you might find that your desires are even more specific or broad! You might want to write a book, travel to fifteen countries, curate a beautiful home, craft an album, grow your business, cut a connection cord, or simply feel at peace. Perhaps you crave more freedom. Welcome and embrace all of it. Unleash your deeper desires.

STEP 2: FEEL IT TO HEAL IT

How do you want to feel?

Next, dive deeper into your desire. How does this desire make you feel? Which of your senses light up when you think about it? Where do you feel this desire in your body? Is it a warm glow in your chest, a tingling in your fingertips, or a sense of calm in your mind? Really explore these sensations and emotions. Write down everything that is alive for you. Surrender the need for your reflection to be perfect or even to make sense; simply write how it feels. You may even include your desire from step 1 to support your feeling statements. In this step, you can freewrite what comes to you or fill in the following prompts.

Journal Prompts:

→ My desire makes me feel _____.

→ Which of my senses lights up: _____

→ Where I feel this desire in my body: _____

Example:

My desire for a job that offers me more money makes me feel capable, free, worthy, proud, excited to wake up every morning, eager to do more, motivated, inspired, safe, and at ease. I feel these sensations as a burst of energy in my heart, expansion in my head, and a tingling sensation in my belly that fires me up!

Here's mine:

> *My desire to write a book makes me feel excited, inspired,*
> *overwhelmed, scared, eager to wake every day, motivated to*
> *do more beyond just the book, open to sharing more of myself,*
> *capable, valuable, relieved, and confident. I feel a burst of*
> *warmth and tingles in my heart, a shuddering in my belly,*
> *and a deep sense of relief in my shoulders and neck.*

Notice that each word embodies a feeling, rather than focusing on a thought or an outcome. Reflecting on a thought might look like this: *My desire for a job that offers me more money makes me feel like I can travel more and pay my bills on time.* In this example, the focus is on manifesting an external outcome rather than an internal state of being. We'll dive deeper into extrinsic versus intrinsic motivation later, but for this exercise, the goal is to clarify how you want to feel in the process toward achieving your desire, not just map out what that desire will get you. We cannot control what happens to us, but we can, to the best of our ability, have a hand in how we feel about it. (Are we starting to see a pattern here, folks?) Get the foundations of feelings down before adding the abundance of thoughts to the mix.

STEP 3: EASE IN

What is your ease?

Feeling excited? Okay, *now* we can amp it up a little.

Shift your focus to the concept of ease. What does ease feel like to you? Picture a life where you move through your days with a sense of grace and tranquility. What do you see? No, literally, what images does your mind create for you? Write these down as if you were writing a page a screenplay or a novel. What does a day in the life of your ease look like? What are you doing? What are you wearing? How do you hold yourself? How do you speak? Who is around you? What sensations do you notice? What does a life of ease mean to you? Write down these feelings and thoughts. Notice if the feelings you reflected on above pop up in your visualization. This is where you get to bring your vision board to life for a moment.

Journal Prompts:

→ To me, a life of ease means _____.

→ For me, a life of ease looks like _____.

I'll give you just a sneak peek at mine:

To me, a life of ease means waking up at the same time every day and being grateful for another day. I recite my daily devotionals, offering verbal gratitude for all the blessings and opportunities that day and my life may grant me. I send my own version of well wishes and gratitude to my loved ones, and I roll out of bed to do a series of light stretches. Once I'm awake and refreshed, I lovingly indulge in my self-care routine before brewing the perfect cup of coffee. I blend the ingredients just right before I head to my desk and set the space. First, I light a candle and incense to brighten up the room. Then, I shake off any nerves or anxiety I might have before sitting down. Finally, I open up the window and my computer, take a deep breath, and let my ideas take form on the page. I smile as I notice the butterflies and birds outside. When I feel I have accomplished a passage that I feel proud of, I reward myself with a breath of fresh air— and maybe a special dinner at my favorite restaurant with a

loved one if I've achieved a major goal. I am proud, fulfilled,
and grateful to be writing this book.

When you're writing out your vision, pay attention to the
details. These minor details have a significant impact on
manifesting your desire into reality. Think of them as the
salt and pepper on your feast of ease—they enhance the
reality you're creating. Let go of judgment, and let your
creativity run wild.

STEP 4: PEN THE PASSION

Craft your Passion Pledge statement.

Once you have all this rich, emotional content laid out in
your journal, it's time to craft your Passion Pledge. This is
where you combine what you desire and how it makes you
feel into a powerful statement—a mantra that will guide
you toward your passion with ease. Your Passion Pledge
should be clear, concise, and deeply personal. It's your
North Star, a reminder of what you're striving for and why
it matters. Look back at your deeper desire, your feelings
of reflection, and your vision of ease. Which sentences or
words stand out the most or make you feel most alive? Take
these words and string them into a single sentence.

When I was writing this book, I crafted the following
Passion Pledge:

> *I pledge to create a book-writing experience that excites me*
> *to wake up in the morning, motivates me to share more*
> *aspects of my life, and fills me with an even deeper gratitude*
> *for being human than ever before.*

This, to me, is ease. I could recite this pledge effortlessly,
had it taped on my office wall, and referred to it anytime

I needed a reminder or a boost to stay on track while writing this (and my next) book. Below, you can see the key components of my single-sentence commitment.

→ **Action:** Creating a book-writing experience based on my desire to write a book

→ **Emotions/Feelings:** Excitement to wake up in the morning because of the physical sensations and visualization of ease

→ **Motivates/Inspires:** Motivates me to confidently share more of myself, driven by the thoughts this book evokes and the outcomes it can lead to

Here is another example:

I pledge to find and secure a job that offers a higher salary, excites me to start each workday, brings me a sense of security, and allows me to enjoy the financial freedom I've visualized. This situation motivates me to excel in my career, contribute more effectively to my team, and continuously grow both professionally and personally.

→ **Action:** Finding and securing a job that offers a higher salary

→ **Feelings/Emotions:** Excites me to start each workday, brings me a sense of security, and fosters joy in financial freedom

→ **Motivates/Inspires:** Motivates me to excel in my career, contribute more effectively to my team, and continuously grow both professionally and personally

STEP 5: MAKE THE PLEDGE

Now, it's your turn.

Passion Pledge Prompt:

I pledge to (action) that (feelings/sensations), which (motivations/inspirations).

Now that you have your Passion Pledge, put it somewhere you can see it every day. Get in the habit of saying and sharing your pledge out loud to yourself and with your trusted support system. Let your pledge blend seamlessly into your daily routine. We'll dive into pledging full allegiance to ourselves later, but for now, with our dish's base simmering nicely, it's time to trim the fat. Choosing ease is just the first step. Next, we'll tackle the self-sabotaging behaviors that love to get in the way of feeling it.

CHAPTER 2

IT'S HARD BEING HUMAN

*"Life is not a problem to be solved, but
a reality to be experienced."*
—Søren Kierkegaard

THE NATURE OF HARDSHIPS

This gem is from my favorite Danish existential philosopher, Søren Kierkegaard. (*What?!* You don't have one?!) This slogan has been bouncing around philosophical circles forever, and it's been paraphrased and riffed on by everyone from Frank Herbert in *Dune* to J.J. van der Leeuw in *The Conquest of Illusion*. The common thread? A fundamental truth about the human experience: life is an adventure to be lived. It's like the thrill you feel when you get a letter right in Wordle or one row in a Rubik's cube. It's not about solving the whole thing at once but rather savoring those small moments of progress. The real joy comes in the unfolding, in each little revelation along the way. Life isn't about nailing the perfect outcome; it's about embracing the journey, celebrating the moments when something clicks, and allowing the rest to reveal itself in time.

Let's dive deep into the nitty-gritty: life is hard. There's no sugarcoating it. No matter who you are, where you come from, or what you do, being human can feel like trying to play a game with a controller you've never used before. Your fingers keep hitting the wrong buttons, and instead of leveling up and exiting through the door on the right, you're just running into the same wall, over and over again. We all face challenges, blocks, and hardships. It's part of the package deal of being human. But here's the twist: these tough times aren't the locked gates to an easy life—they're the *keys* to a life of ease. They push us to evolve. Think about it: wars, economic depressions, social upheavals—each one, despite its pain, has nudged humanity forward, creating ease for future generations. But let's not get bogged down in history; this is about your journey.

THE HUMAN CONDITION

Let's stick with the existential perspective for a second. The human condition is inherently a condition of being alive—a roller coaster filled with love, suffering, and everything in between. Just like describing a friend in poor health, the word "condition" captures our state of conscious being. The political theorist Hannah Arendt explained the term "the human condition" in her 1958 book of the same name, which explores the wild journey of being human and what we're capable of doing. Even though Arendt gave us this catchy label, the general concept has been around forever. Every generation has tried to wrap its head around what it means to be human. Sure, we're all unique with our own identities, backgrounds, races, genders—the list goes on. Some argue that there can't be just one human condition with all these differences. But the human condition isn't about erasing our differences. It's about recognizing what we have in common.

There are aspects of living that each human will experience no matter what—growing up, love, death, friendship, and maturation. Our differences color these aspects of life and show them in different lights, but at their core, they're shared human experiences. There's always that age-old question: Is the "human condition" a serious affliction to be endured or a privilege to be cherished? It's both. At the drop of a hat, we can navigate a whirlwind of emotions (some better than others). We can choose to keep our feelings and thoughts locked away in our private mental vaults or share our stories with trusted others. This sharing helps soothe that existential dread we all have—the fear of not living the "right" way and constantly questioning if we're doing "it" right.

Now, our human condition is a bit like a vitamin B_{12} shot: it offers psychological, social, physical, and spiritual nourishment, but whether it's a shot in the arm or in the butt, it's uncomfortable and slightly distressing. If there were a quick fix for clarity and simplicity, we'd all jump at the chance despite the initial discomfort. (And no, I'm not talking about numbing yourself with meds or substances.) From my psychology background, I understand that some conditions require medication and therapy, but this book tackles the broader, existential aspects of being human. We can't cure the human condition; we can only navigate and fully experience it.

This understanding of the human condition brings us to a crucial aspect of our human hardships: our limiting beliefs and self-sabotaging behaviors. You see, the blocks we encounter—the ones that whisper we're not good enough, capable enough, or worthy enough—are part of that shared human experience. These limiting beliefs are like stubborn stains on the fabric of our consciousness, embedded deep from past experiences, societal conditioning, or even generational patterns. They're not just random thoughts; they're woven into the very fabric of our existence, making them a core part of our human condition.

Life Lesson: While we can't escape the human condition, we can learn to navigate it with more ease by addressing these blocks head-on. In the same way we experience other universal aspects of life, we also universally grapple with beliefs that limit us. And just as we can choose how to respond to the broader challenges of being human, we can choose how to engage with these limiting beliefs. Either we can let them control our narrative, or we can confront them, understand their roots, and ultimately transform them into superpowers instead of kryptonite.

So, as we move forward, let's acknowledge that these blocks—these limiting beliefs—are just part of the package deal of being human. They're not flaws or signs of failure; they're invitations to deepen our understanding of ourselves and redefine our relationship with the human condition. By addressing them, we're not just making life easier; we're engaging in the very essence of what it means to be authentically human.

SELF-SABOTAGING BEHAVIOR AND LIMITING BELIEFS

Before we dive deeper, allow me to clarify what I mean by self-sabotaging behavior. Self-sabotage refers to actions or thoughts that undermine our own success and happiness. It's like planting weeds in our garden and wondering why the flowers struggle to grow. These behaviors can manifest in various ways—procrastination, negative self-talk, or setting unrealistic goals, to name a few. For example, if you consistently put off important tasks, you're sabotaging your own progress. Or if you always tell yourself you're not good enough, you're setting up roadblocks on your path to success. These behaviors often stem from deeply rooted limiting beliefs.

Limiting beliefs are the negative thoughts and convictions that hold us back. They are the mental blocks that tell us we're not good enough, not ready, or don't deserve success. Think of them as the invisible chains that keep a dragon tethered to the ground when it's trying to soar (look out for chapter 7 of my next book). These beliefs tell you things like "I'm not smart enough," "I'm not ready," or "I don't deserve success." If you believe that success is only for other people, you might not even try to pursue your dreams, because you've already convinced yourself that achieving them is impossible. These beliefs are often ingrained in us from past experiences or societal conditioning. Understanding self-sabotaging behavior and limiting beliefs is crucial because they explain why we sometimes feel stuck or unable to achieve our goals.

For years, I clung to a limiting belief that revolved around a fear of success: "I'm not capable of managing and sustaining large-scale success." While many grapple with a fear of failure, mine was "What if I succeed?" Instead of focusing on the positive outcomes, I fixated on the negative aspects: sacrificing quality time with loved ones, compromising personal pleasures, maintaining success, and being seen. Somehow, these fears scared me more than failing. Failure became my comfort zone, like that soothing glass of wine I mentioned earlier, while success felt like a daunting tequila shot.

Because of this fear, my self-sabotaging behavior was to play small and do less. I stuck to smaller arenas where, due to the lower stakes, success was almost guaranteed but also didn't launch me to my full potential. Ironically, when I look back now, I see a laundry list of success stories and big risks. However, I also recognize how long it took me to actualize my bigger goals. My default avoidance and dissociation delayed my progress and kept me from applying myself authentically. I finally identified what wasn't working and made choices that acknowledged these fears but weren't guided by them. When I was kinder to myself, life got easier. But before I reveal one of those success stories, let me break down how I handled the hardships.

IDENTIFYING PERSONAL OBSTACLES

Have you considered what is blocking your desire, standing in the way of your success, and reminding you of what you don't have? It's crucial to become aware of and compassionately confront your personal obstacles. I'm calling out that mental voice that whispers (or sometimes shouts) that we're not good enough, not ready, or don't deserve to succeed. It's like the uninvited party guest who just won't leave.

Limiting beliefs are often deeply ingrained, born from past experiences or societal conditioning. But by spotting these blocks and calling them out, we can turn them into our stepstones to level up. It's like playing Whac-A-Mole, bopping limiting beliefs and negative thoughts the second they attempt to interfere with your confidence. And guess what? Each bop clears the way for a little more progress and a lot more ease. If you're thinking, *Easier said than done*, don't worry: we're in this together. I promise that once you get past the initial groan of doing the "work," it will become a natural process of identifying your blocks and patterns! (Because who doesn't love getting cozy with their insecurities?)

Remember, it's all part of the recipe for a more fulfilling life. Let's find those ingredients, toss out what doesn't serve us, and keep cooking up some deliciously easy living! (Should we start an analogy drinking game now or what?)

When we choose the path of least resistance, we might avoid immediate discomfort, but we also miss out on the opportunities embedded in challenges. It's in the struggle that we find our strength. Consider the butterfly emerging from its chrysalis. The struggle to break free strengthens its wings and prepares it for flight. Without that struggle, the butterfly would never soar. Similarly, our hardships force us to grow and develop resilience.

Take a moment to reflect on your own experience. Visualize a time when life felt hard. Really hard. Like, how-am-I-going-to-get-through-this hard. Really let yourself go there. What made it so challenging? Was it something happening outside of yourself that you couldn't control? Or was it an internal struggle that interfered with your goals and intentions?

Confronted with these questions, maybe an image effortlessly popped into your head, or maybe you drew a blank. Right now, without any excuses or rationalizations getting in the way, ask yourself: *Why don't I have my deeper desire?* You crafted your Passion Pledge in chapter 1, so why isn't it already your reality? If you find yourself compelled to list the practical reasons why your desire is out of reach, I validate you. But I also challenge you to reexamine your list and see if there is a deeper truth beneath the circumstances. If you don't have enough money, why? If you don't have the partner of your dreams, why? If you don't love your life, *why?!*

BEFRIENDING OUR BLOCKS

Before potential panic sets in, let's take this opportunity to notice what comes up when you ask yourself some tough questions. Do you have a deeper knowing of what is standing in the way? Can you hear that little voice trying to tell you something? Does a pattern of behaviors reveal itself when you ask those heart-pounding questions? If so, that's positive! You've just identified a roadblock! Now let's make friends with it.

There will be a time when we dive into the dreamy visualizations of our desires, but for the sake of unmasking your blocks, let's revisit what you discovered about your personal obstacles. This might be a little challenging, as our human nature often overrides our ability to hold space for perceived failure. But instead of seeing these blocks as failures, just observe them. Hold space for them like you would for that friend at a party who's venting about their relationship drama. You might see the truth clearly as the observer, but the person experiencing the drama usually can't see what's standing in their way. This is your chance to objectively hold space for your blocks (and hold off on the critical input).

Maybe you equate ease with your ideal life partner. So why don't you have that person? There is an answer if you're willing to claim it. Perhaps you're not ready for the relationship you envision. Maybe you don't know what you truly want in a partner. Perhaps you're avoidant or anxious. Maybe your self-control wavers when making mature decisions. Remember, this is a no-judgment zone! The point is to understand there's a reason your deeper desires are not your reality. You might be contributing something to the equation that's keeping you from getting what you want. There is a reason life feels so hard.

If you're struggling to identify your block, don't worry—
you're not alone. It's not always easy to spot what's
holding you back, especially when the barriers are deeply
ingrained. If you're finding it difficult to pinpoint your
block, start by getting curious about your thoughts and
behaviors. Notice any patterns that keep popping up. Are
there areas of your life where you consistently feel stuck,
frustrated, or disappointed? Sometimes, blocks hide
behind familiar excuses or repeated habits. If nothing
comes to mind right away, give yourself permission to sit
with the discomfort and ask the tough questions again.
What are you afraid of? What would you do if you weren't
afraid? Sometimes, the block just waits for a little bit of
attention before it reveals itself.

And if you're still unsure, it's okay to reach out for support—
whether that's a trusted friend, a therapist, or a coach (I
got you!) who can help you see what's hidden. Though
it might feel a bit uncomfortable at first, asking for an
outside perspective can be incredibly helpful in identifying
what you might not see about yourself. Establishing trust
and confidentiality with a reliable source allows you to
ask these tough questions and receive feedback about the
behaviors or patterns others might notice in you. These
sources can also help you spot recurring themes or
emotions that you consistently vent about. It's not always
easy to spot the thorn on the rose, but when we slow down
to examine it, we're left with something truly beautiful.

Hopefully, now you've spotted the block and noticed
what's standing between you and the ease you desire. So,
as you would with a friend, give this block some room to
vent. The block is there for a reason. It is trying to tell you
something. It's trying to bring something deeper to your
attention. So, if your block were to give you its side of the
story, what would that sound like? This isn't about making
it a main course but rather giving it an appetizer's worth

of attention. When clients feel stuck or lack clarity, I often suggest talking to their feelings. If you're feeling sad, talk to the sadness and let it talk back (full-on *Inside Out* style). It will often tell you what it needs. Ask your block why it's there and what it believes.

Maybe your block's belief system is deeply rooted in your subconscious, developed to protect you from perceived dangers. Asking your block what it believes may reveal an irrational or impractical story, but does it still feel true? Let's take the relationship example: If the block is avoidance and you ask it what it believes, the block might say, "Avoiding deeper issues and bigger feelings seems easier than confronting or communicating through them. If we talk about our feelings, I might not be able to handle them, and you might see I'm weak or incapable!"

The block believes avoiding intimacy keeps you safe. The block is avoidance, and it wants safety. It thinks it's helping you! It operates under the notion that it is providing you with something you wouldn't have otherwise. You can now identify how your hardship is actually trying to help you.

Let's start by befriending the block with compassion and empathy. Acknowledge the block with gratitude for its attempt to fulfill a deeper need, even if its approach wasn't helpful. Then, gently ask it to step aside. Doesn't that feel better? By treating our blocks as friends instead of foes, we create a pathway to ease. We transform resistance into understanding and, ultimately, growth. What's more, we embrace ease by seeing the opportunity in the block, not just the hardship. Even though, at times, it feels like your blocks are working against you, befriending your blocks is an obstacle remover that can unveil a pathway to your purpose. So, what do you do after you've befriended your blocks?

REFRAME TO RECLAIM

Let's dive into the "Reframe to Reclaim" method, which is all about transforming your hardships into opportunities and shifting your mindset toward positivity. This practice creates ease by focusing on the positive possibilities rather than dwelling on negative beliefs. This process supports you in reclaiming your truth, revitalizing your authenticity, and reconnecting you with your initial intention or the powerful "why" behind your desire for a more ease-filled life.

STEP 1: AWARENESS OF NEGATIVE PATTERNS

First, you need to become aware of the negative thoughts or patterns holding you back. Identify these thoughts and recognize them for what they are—blocks in your path.

Example:

> *You realize you often think, I'm not good enough to get that promotion.*

STEP 2: EXPRESS GRATITUDE FOR AWARENESS

Once you've identified these thoughts, express gratitude for the awareness. As accomplished motivational author and speaker Gabby Bernstein mentions in her "Choose Again" method, thanking unwanted thoughts helps you identify what you truly desire. Similarly, in the Reframe to Reclaim method, recognizing and thanking these hardships allows you to see the lessons behind them.

This step is about acknowledging and appreciating the awareness of the negative thought or pattern. It's the act of recognizing that you've identified something that needs to be addressed and being thankful for the insight it provides. This is an important step because it shifts your mindset from seeing these negative thoughts as purely detrimental to recognizing them as indicators of areas for growth. This awareness is a necessary *emotional* step toward reframing your blocks, as gratitude creates space for acceptance.

Example:

> *I'm grateful that I've become aware of my "I'm not good enough" thought, because this awareness is the first step toward positive change. Recognizing this pattern helps me see where I can refocus my efforts toward greater ease and happiness.*

STEP 3: REFRAME YOUR HARDSHIPS

Reframing is all about viewing your hardships as opportunities for growth. Instead of seeing these challenges as roadblocks, consider what they might be teaching you. Here, you actively change your perspective on the identified negative thought or pattern. This shift in perspective can transform obstacles into secret ingredients. This step highlights the mental acceptance in the reframing process that sets you up for taking aligned action.

Example:

> *Rather than seeing the lack of a promotion as a failure, view it as an opportunity to level up to your highest self. Tell yourself, These thoughts are teaching me that I can improve my self-confidence and celebrate my achievements by improving my skills and showcasing my value more effectively.*

In essence, step 2 is about appreciating the awareness of the problem, while step 3 is about transforming that problem into a learning opportunity or a chance to grow.

STEP 4: CONSCIOUS SELF-RELEASE

Here, we borrow a concept from my mentor Alyssa Nobriga, a renowned life coach and speaker who notes compassionate self-forgiveness is a crucial step in any process. I have found that conscious self-release embodies this sentiment by not only actively forgiving but also consciously releasing yourself from the belief systems, blocks, and patterns that have held you back from your desired feelings. This practice frees you from the shame, guilt, doubt, or judgment associated with these defense mechanisms and is the next step toward unlocking the subconscious doors you may have shut within yourself.

Example:

> *I release myself from the belief that I am not good enough for a promotion. The truth is, I am capable and continue to grow in my career.*

STEP 5: RECLAIM YOUR TRUTH

You have now given yourself permission to change. You have moved through awareness and acceptance, and into aligned action, by releasing yourself from the chain of the blocks that you believed kept you safe. With this freedom, you get to expand. After releasing and forgiving yourself for holding on to these blocks, return to gratitude. Thank the process for revealing what your focus gets to be now. This is where you reclaim your truth. Acknowledge the belief that gets you closer to your deeper desire and the life of ease you seek.

Example:

> *Thank you, belief, for highlighting my desire to advance in my career. I now focus on enhancing my skills and demonstrating my value to secure that promotion. I know what I want, and I get to claim it now.*

Now—you guessed it—it's your turn! Half the battle in confronting hardships is doing something about them. Use the following template, here or on the downloadable worksheet, to reframe a block or hardship and reclaim your power. Take this tool and let it be easy!

REFRAME TO RECLAIM PROMPTS

Step 1: Awareness of Negative Patterns

→ Identify the negative thought or pattern holding you back: *The negative thought or pattern I am currently aware of is _____.*

Step 2: Express Gratitude for Awareness

→ Express gratitude for recognizing this negative thought or pattern: *I am grateful for recognizing this thought/pattern because it shows me _____.*

Step 3: Reframe Your Hardships

→ Consider what this hardship might be teaching you: *This thought/pattern is teaching me that I need to _____.*

Step 4: Conscious Self-Release

→ Release yourself from the limiting belief with a statement: *I release myself from the belief that _____. The truth is: _____.*

Step 5: Reclaim Your Truth

→ Thank the thought for revealing your true needs and refocus on your deeper desire: *Thank you, (negative belief), for showing me that what I truly need is _____. I now focus on _____.*

GRADUAL GRADUATION

I have relied on the Reframe to Reclaim method my entire life, even before I coined the catchphrase (although I'm sure I'm not the first, but it's my book, so...). I find myself leaning on it almost every day for its ability to take the pressure off the hardships and realign me with pathways of ease. In chapter 1, I set the scene for how I ended up where I am today. Accepting ease into my life as an adult meant stepping away from my adolescent dream of being a famous (or, let's face it, at least a working) actress. Of course, there were inherent obstacles and hardships before and during this moment. But let's talk about what happened after I chose ease and my blocks intervened. It's hard being human, even when you get what you want—sometimes especially then. When I got accepted to Pepperdine University to pursue my master's in psychology, I felt a huge sense of accomplishment. Leaving behind a burdensome acting career, I stepped toward a path that aligned with my values and authentic joy. I wanted to help people, be of service, and get paid for it. I craved the credibility and credentials of a professional. I wanted to be successful.

Initially, grad school felt like any school experience—manageable at the start but increasingly challenging as it progressed. The first year was a balancing act of working in entertainment to fulfill previous commitments while maintaining good grades. Then, the pandemic hit during my second and final year, and everything changed. My motivation, resilience, and inspiration started to wane. Schoolwork became harder, and the pressure of lockdown life made everything feel overwhelming. During this time, I had countless vulnerable conversations with my counselor about how to navigate these feelings. Eventually, I decided to take a semester off, a choice that set me back enough to extend my graduation by a year.

I felt incapable, lazy, and stupid for not keeping up with my classmates. My focus dissipated, my motivation fizzled, and my desire was burning out. I felt like a failure for needing a break. My block is believing I am not capable—that I must be perfect and excel the first time I try something. I am a Leo, after all. And a Manifesting Generator. And a seven in the Enneagram. Basically, all signs point toward a belief in self-excellence. Yet I still manage to convince myself that I am not capable of doing things I don't know how to do! Being a beginner? Shocking! Learning how to do something new? I'd rather quit. And countless times, I have.

Part of my block of believing I am not capable is believing I am not worthy of my own success. The fear of success has haunted me, convincing me that maintaining it would be impossible. I approach the world in an open-hearted, free-spirited, and fiercely self-critical manner. These qualities tend to be the attributes that others praise me for, yet they also seem to be the traits that stand in my way. My process to achieve success has always appeared different from what I have seen in standard settings. The education system was always hard for me.

This brought back memories of my freshman year of high school, when I was diagnosed with ADHD and transferred to a slower math class, which I perceived as being where the "dumb kids" were placed. I felt different, and different seemed bad. I couldn't control how my brain processed certain information like math, and this lack of control made me feel unworthy of learning. My block told me it was easier to accept failure, so I wouldn't ask for help or support. I convinced myself that I would never learn, so why bother trying?

However, once I was in the intermediate class, I realized the benefits. I thrived in a less pressured environment, learning alongside peers who also needed more time to process. My teacher, in his older age, reveled in breaking down each algorithm with positive reinforcement. (At the time, it felt like a snail's pace, but it also felt comforting, and who wouldn't love a Starburst for raising your hand?) This was, and remains to this day, the only class in which I have received a genuine 100 percent, a bona fide A+. Remembering this experience, I realized I was buying into the belief that to be valued I had to stick to a standard timeline and push myself beyond breaking. But maybe, just maybe, taking time off was actually a smart choice. By giving myself the time and space to learn at my own pace, I could absorb the education fully rather than punishing myself for not keeping up.

In grad school, I felt like a failure for needing a break, a belief that traced back to high school. Despite successfully navigating that earlier challenge, when I moved to a slower math class and initially felt judged, the negative belief lingered. I felt grateful for recognizing this negative pattern; I acknowledged it. I said to my block, Thank you for showing me that I feel inadequate when I don't follow the conventional timeline. Instead of viewing taking a break as a failure, I saw it as a strategic move to give myself the space to learn effectively. I reframed it: Taking a break allows me to fully absorb my education and come back stronger. I released the guilt and judgment I held against myself: I gently release myself from the belief that I am not capable because I need a break. The truth is, I am deserving of time and space to learn at my own pace. I thanked the block for revealing my true needs: Thank you for showing me my need for a slower and extended process when learning and taking on new things. I now focus on creating space and time for myself, as well as not burning out, by balancing my priorities.

So, I took that semester off. It took me three years to graduate instead of two. But when I returned, I was refreshed and refocused. I finished grad school with honors, beaming as I walked up to receive my diploma, hearing my name on the dean's list, and waving to the crowd. I wasn't stupid! I was capable! I wanted to learn and participate! I wanted to succeed, and I just needed a different process! I was different! And it's hard being different. But everyone is different; that's the point. There isn't one "right" way to do anything. Life is about understanding what you need and figuring out how to meet those needs.

That's the point of this chapter—it's hard being human, and everyone feels this! The hardships are different, but the feelings are the same! Pain is pain. But here's the **Life Lesson:** the way you choose to see your pain and interpret your hardships is a reflection of how you choose to love and care for yourself. When you acknowledge your struggles without judgment and approach them with compassion, you're practicing self-love. When you choose to see your struggles as opportunities to understand and support yourself, you're choosing to celebrate rather than criticize yourself. This means acknowledging your challenges without harsh judgment and instead approaching them with kindness and care. Do you want life to be harder? Likely not, since you're still reading this book and all.

There may always be something standing in your way. That's life. As you grow, your blocks may grow with you. But releasing those blocks and finding ease in your journey is possible—if you let it be! So now that you're more aware of what you don't want, it's time to put your money where your mouth is and start investing in what you do want.

PART 2

THE SYNERGY OF SELF-INVESTMENT

If life's a stage and ease is the story,
you are the main character.

(CHAPTER 3

THE SECRET OF SELF-INVESTMENT

"Acceptance is a process that we experience, not a final stage with an end point."

—Elisabeth Kübler-Ross,
On Grief and Grieving

SELF-INVESTMENT AND WHY IT MATTERS

We've tackled the difference between ease and easy, confronted your blocks, and explored how to reframe them. Now, with a clearer sense of the life you desire, it's time to dive into self-investment. By reading this, you've already started unlocking this essential ingredient. Life gets to be easy if you let it, and self-investment is central to that dynamic. Self-investment is like cooking a gourmet meal for yourself instead of grabbing fast food. It's about recognizing that you deserve the best ingredients—time, effort, and care. Investment isn't just about finances; it's about attending to your growth, well-being, and authenticity. It's about saying, "I'm worth the good stuff." When I began writing this book, I revisited the tough moments in my life—just like I asked you to do in chapter

2. That process revealed a timeline of choices driven by how I wanted to feel. At every point, my decisions boiled down to acceptance—of myself, my desires, and my path. Some choices were far from practical, but they led me to a life I'm deeply proud of because they were true to me.

Life Lesson: the secret of self-investment is acceptance. In a world that profits from self-doubt, liking yourself is a radical act. No one can define ease or authenticity for you but you. Listening to yourself and making choices aligned with your inner knowing is when life starts to get easier.

Remember, self-investment is continuous. It's not a one-time deal but rather a process of regularly checking in with yourself, understanding your needs, and making decisions that support your growth. Acceptance is the pulse of this process. As long as we are alive, we are in a state of wanting and needing. If we can't accept what is true for our well-being, life gets harder. People often admire me for knowing who I am, but what they're really seeing is self-acceptance. Getting to know myself meant accepting the parts I didn't like and trusting that I could live with my choices. It wasn't easy—I've felt silly, insecure, and confused more times than I care to admit. But I own it now. Self-investment means embracing self-acceptance, and it's in these moments that the path to ease is revealed. The choices you make reflect who you are at your core. So, are you ready to accept who you are and invest in the abundance you crave? Good. Let's keep going.

THE INSIDE-OUT APPROACH

Self-investment is all about working from the inside out. It's the cooking process, not the eating; what you put into the pot and how you feel in the kitchen will impact the final flavor. Have you ever heard of chefs singing or reciting loving sentiments into their food? Or have you heard of people who tell their plants they love them? Science says it works! The diner is happier, and the plant grows stronger! (*Holistic pro tip:* If you love your food, your food will love you.) In the next chapter, we'll dive into intrinsic versus extrinsic motivation (remember that psychology degree I mentioned?). But for now, let's stick with the idea that real, lasting change starts within. This inside-out approach means that the choices you make are driven by how you want to feel during the process, not just by the outcome you're chasing. It's about savoring the journey rather than fixating on the destination.

The outside-in approach, on the other hand, can be misleading. It promises that external achievements will make you feel the way you want to feel inside. For example, a classic outside-in mindset is thinking, *Once I get that job, I'll be happy.* But here's the twist: What if you flipped it around? What if you decided to cultivate happiness within yourself first and then watched how it transformed your life, leading you to a job you love? That's the magic of working from the inside out.

Now, acceptance might be the secret ingredient in our recipe for ease, but let's break down the whole recipe for self-investment into three key ingredients I learned from my mentor, Alyssa Nobriga: awareness, acceptance, and aligned action. These foundational elements will help you cook up a life that feels nourishing, satisfying, and authentically yours.

AWARENESS

Awareness is like taking inventory of your life's pantry. Before you start cooking up your dream life, you need to know which ingredients you have on hand. What are your strengths? Where do you want to grow? This step involves honest self-reflection and a clear-eyed look at your current reality. Are there expired beliefs cluttering your shelves, taking up space, and keeping you from making room for something better? Maybe you've got some fresh talents you haven't fully tapped into yet.

Awareness is all about recognizing what you're working with and what you need. It's realizing that you want to take a chance or that something isn't working for you. It's noticing the patterns, blocks, and self-sabotaging behaviors that keep you feeling lost or stuck. It's also observing what you love and what you're good at (there's a name for that—stay tuned!). It's the first step toward ensuring your recipe for life is on point.

ACCEPTANCE

Acceptance is like tasting your dish as you cook. You might realize it needs more salt, but that doesn't mean the dish is ruined—it just means you're refining it. Acceptance is about embracing where you are right now, without judgment. It's understanding that every part of your journey is a vital ingredient in your life's recipe. You're not settling for less; you're acknowledging your worth and potential, even if things aren't perfect.

Acceptance is an active process—it's the seasoning that brings out the best in your life, adding depth, flavor, and richness to your experiences. Acceptance is the secret ingredient, because only you possess the truth about who you genuinely are. No one else can define you, and that's what makes it so powerful. When you truly accept yourself—your strengths, your flaws, your quirks—you're not just adding flavor to your life; you're ensuring it's authentic to your taste. This step is about honoring your individuality and using it as a foundation to build the life you want. Embrace it, season it, and let it simmer into something uniquely yours. If *you* accept who you are, no one can take that acceptance away from you. And when you fully own it, you might just find that everyone around you wants a taste. (Your special sauce is its own chapter for a reason.)

ALiGNED ACTiON

Now that you've taken inventory and seasoned your life with acceptance, it's time for aligned action. This is where you start cooking up the life you want, adding the right ingredients at the right time. Aligned action is about putting your intentions into practice—following through on what you've set out to do. It's the deliberate choice to move in harmony with your goals and values, ensuring that each step you take is purposeful and directed. Think of it like following a recipe: each action, no matter how small, contributes to the final masterpiece. And just like cooking, sometimes you need to adjust on the fly, adding a little more of this or that to get the flavor just right. But as long as you're moving forward with intention and integrity, you're on the right track.

By breaking down self-investment into awareness, acceptance, and aligned action, you're equipping yourself with a solid foundation for building a life that's not only fulfilling but also genuinely easier. You're not just going through the motions; you're actively creating a life that reflects your true self, and that's the key to unlocking lasting ease and joy. You'll find yourself more open to experimenting with behaviors and belief systems that move you closer to your deeper desires—whether it's landing your dream job, building epic relationships, making more money, or finding inner peace. Awareness and acceptance will be your compass, guiding you to take actions that align with what you truly want.

PUT YOUR MONEY WHERE YOUR MOUTH IS

Here's where the rubber meets the road in self-investment: actually doing what you say you're going to do. It's easy to talk about the changes you want to make or the goals you want to achieve, but the real challenge lies in the follow-through. Do you keep the promises you make to yourself? In a life of ease, not only do you follow through on what you say you're going to do, you also live in a way that reflects your true values and intentions. When you start aligning your actions with who you genuinely are, something magical happens. You begin to invest in yourself on all levels—money, intention, time, and energy. And you begin to get more of those resources in return.

"Put your money where your mouth is" is a reminder that real commitment often requires putting some skin in the game. Whether it's enrolling in a course to fuel your growth, investing in therapy to nurture your mental health, or simply dedicating time to pursue your passions, these actions are all powerful forms of self-investment. Each one sends a clear signal to the universe—and, more importantly, to yourself—that you are committed to your growth and well-being. When you start living in authentic alignment with who you are, you might find that wealth and opportunity flow more naturally into your life. It's not just wishful thinking; it's a practical outcome of living in your truth.

When you're clear about what you want and committed to your path, you create a magnetic energy that attracts the right opportunities, connections, and yes, even financial abundance. It's possible—if not inevitable—that by living in alignment with your authentic self, you'll find yourself not just richer in experience but potentially wealthier in a very tangible way. So, as we dive into this section on self-investment, remember the **Life Lesson:** every action you take in alignment with your true self is a powerful investment in your future. (Don't stress; we'll add some practical investments later.)

Think of self-investment as the decision to cook and pick out the best recipe to follow. You've gathered the best ingredients (awareness, acceptance, and aligned action), and now it's time to cook. Honoring promises to yourself is like making sure each step in the recipe is executed with care and intention. If you skip steps or substitute ingredients haphazardly, the final dish won't turn out as expected. The same goes for your personal growth: if you don't follow through on your commitments, you're shortchanging yourself and undermining your progress.

Let's break this principle down with a few examples. Say you've set a goal to exercise three times a week to improve your health. You start out strong, but then life gets busy, and you skip a workout. The next week, it's easier to skip two, and soon, you're back to square one. Each time you break a promise to yourself, it chips away at your confidence and self-respect. You start to doubt whether you can achieve your goals at all.

On the flip side, when you do what you say you're going to do, you build trust with yourself.

But what happens when the going gets tough? What happens when that initial excitement fades and you're faced with the real work, the part where change feels uncomfortable or progress seems slow? This is when many people stumble. It's when you're tested—when your commitment to yourself is challenged. This is when you let it get hard.

So, how do you push past this struggle? First, remind yourself why you started. When my clients seem lost in their pursuits, I say, "Remember your why!" At times, when I was writing this book, I'd get lost in trying to curate the perfect sentence or dish out another analogy (I accept my cringe!). But then I reminded myself that I embarked on this project because I wanted to offer others the life lessons I wish I'd learned earlier on. I wanted to share my work and the ideas that helped shape a life I am proud to be living. My why was to simply write a book. I returned to this fact anytime the writing process stumped me or life intervened and made the production of this book harder. Over time, my why got deeper and stronger. And it supported me in putting my money where my mouth is (catch the Easter egg title yet?). Reconnect with the deeper desires that motivated you in the first place. Visualize the outcome you're striving for, whether it's a healthier body, a more fulfilling career, or inner peace. This visualization can reignite your motivation and help you push through the discomfort.

Next, break down your goals into smaller, more manageable steps. If the thought of committing to a full workout routine feels overwhelming, start with just ten minutes a day. Success builds on success, and each small win will make it easier to tackle the next challenge. Finally, practice self-compassion. Understand that slipups are part of the process, not the end of it. Instead of beating yourself up for missing a workout or falling short of your goal, acknowledge the lapse, forgive yourself, and get back on track. Self-investment isn't about perfection; it's about progress.

This is the meat and potatoes of self-investment: loving yourself enough to support your growth through consistent, intentional action. When you keep your word to yourself, you're not just making progress toward your goals—you're building a stronger, more resilient self who knows that you're capable of achieving whatever you set your mind to. Let's deep-dive into some reflection and see if you're putting your money where your mouth is.

STEP 1: WHAT DO YOU WANT?

This is where the real work of self-investment begins. In a sense, we have to talk the talk before we walk the walk. So we have to begin with awareness: What is your mouth saying? What is your *why*? This step is about reminding yourself why you want what you want so it can motivate you to do something about it.

→ **Action:** Identify a specific commitment you've made to yourself or an intention you set. It could be starting a new habit (like exercising regularly) or taking steps toward a personal goal (like writing a book or launching a project).

→ **Reflection:** What do you want in life? Why do you believe it will make you happier, more at peace, or more successful? What do you believe it will give you that you don't already have? What is your life like without it?

STEP 2: BREAK IT DOWN

Honoring promises to yourself is like executing each step in the recipe with care and intention. If you skip steps or make careless substitutions, the final dish won't turn out as expected. Similarly, if you don't follow through on your commitments, you're undermining your progress and self-trust.

> → **Action:** Revisit your goals and break them down into smaller, more manageable steps. What do you need to do in order to achieve your goal or honor your promise? For example, if your goal is to exercise more, start with a commitment of ten minutes a day rather than an hour.

> → **Reflection:** Reflect on how it feels when you follow through on a commitment. What positive emotions arise? How does it impact your self-esteem and belief in your ability to achieve your goals? When you break it down, how does it feel to see what you are capable of or have control over? Is there a deeper acceptance of what you cannot control or where you are in the process?

STEP 3: CELEBRATE THE SMALL STUFF

Each time you keep a promise to yourself, you're building trust and confidence. This trust is crucial because it's the foundation of your self-esteem and belief in your ability to achieve your desires. Every time you follow through, you reinforce the idea that you are capable and worthy of success.

> → **Action:** Create a daily or weekly check-in ritual to review your progress and acknowledge the commitments you've honored. Celebrate these small wins, as they are the building blocks of greater success.

> → **Reflection:** How does your trust in yourself grow as you consistently follow through on

your commitments? What new opportunities or challenges are you now more willing to take on? How do you celebrate yourself? What rituals, habits, or practices are you willing to experiment with to feel the positive reinforcement of your efforts and wins? Do you forsake the small moments, thinking they are insignificant to the grander success you crave? How does your daily life change when you make space for self-celebration?

STEP 4: REMEMBER YOUR WHY

When the initial excitement fades and you're faced with the real work, the part where change feels uncomfortable, or progress seems slow, your commitment to yourself is challenged.

→ **Action:** When you hit a rough patch, reconnect with your why. Visualize the outcome you're striving for—whether it's a healthier body, a fulfilling career, or inner peace. Use this visualization to reignite your motivation. Identify a challenge you're currently facing and think about how reconnecting with your why can help you push through it.

→ **Reflection:** Why do you want what you want? Why do you believe your goal or intention will benefit or enhance your life? What deeper desire fuels your commitment to this goal? Why is it important, if not imperative, for you to actualize this goal or intention? Who are you without this desire? Why are you the person meant to make this intention real?

STEP 5: REFRAME TO RECLAIM

Understand that slipups are part of the process, not the end of it. Instead of beating yourself up for missing a workout or falling short of a goal, acknowledge the lapse, forgive yourself, and get back on track. Self-investment isn't about perfection; it's about progress.

→ **Action:** Develop a self-compassion ritual. When you stumble, take a moment to pause, acknowledge the challenge, and offer yourself kind words of encouragement: *I'm human, and it's okay to make mistakes. I'm still moving forward.*

→ **Reflection:** Looking back at the concepts of reframing to reclaim and conscious self-release from chapter 2, how can you compassionately let go of the self-sabotaging beliefs and habits that stand in your way? How can you forgive yourself? What is the truth about the situation if you were to break it down? What is your truth? How can you reframe to reclaim your power in the process? Reflect on a time when you were hard on yourself for not meeting a goal. How might practicing self-compassion have changed the outcome or your feelings about it?

STEP 6: INTEGRATE INTEGRITY

This journey of self-investment is about loving yourself enough to support your growth through consistent, intentional action. When you keep your word to yourself, you're not just making progress toward your goals—you're building a stronger, more resilient self who knows that you're capable of achieving whatever you set your mind to.

→ **Action:** Revisit your Passion Pledge from chapter 1. Do you need to update or revise this statement of deeper desire? Make sure your pledge outlines your commitment to yourself and your goals. Now, post it somewhere visible as a daily reminder of your promise to yourself. Maybe you tape it to your bathroom mirror, on the fridge, or as your phone background. Place it somewhere you won't ignore it.

→ **Reflection:** How does it feel to do what you say you are going to do? Do you notice acceptance or avoidance when you look at your Passion Pledge? Where do you feel this reaction, and how are you willing to integrate this awareness into aligned action? What results do you notice as you build a stronger foundation of self-trust?

THE RIPPLE EFFECT

After you've put your money where your mouth is, something extraordinary happens: you start to see the ripple effect of your self-investment. It's like dropping a stone into a pond and watching as the ripples spread outward, touching everything in their path. When you invest in yourself, those ripples affect everything and everyone around you. See the power of the inside-out approach? Waves don't happen without something creating them. Your self-love, growth, and commitment to living authentically don't just stay contained within you; they extend outward, influencing your relationships, career, and overall sense of well-being.

Think of it this way: when you make a decision to prioritize your mental health, whether through therapy, meditation, or simply taking time for yourself, the benefits don't stop with you. You become more patient with others, better equipped to handle stress, and more present in your relationships. Suddenly, your partner, friends, and even coworkers notice the change. They see the calmness in your approach, the kindness in your interactions, and the positivity you bring into the room.

Let's say you invest time in developing a new skill, like taking a course to advance your career. Not only do you gain new knowledge and confidence, you also inspire those around you to pursue their own growth. Your dedication might encourage a friend to finally start that project they've been putting off, or it might motivate a colleague to step up in their own role. This is the ripple effect in action. Your growth becomes a beacon for others, showing them what's possible when you commit to self-investment.

And it doesn't stop there. The more you invest in yourself, the more you align with your true desires and values, which often leads to a more fulfilling and successful career. This success isn't just about financial gain (though that might come too); it's about finding work that resonates with who you are, work that brings you joy and purpose. And when you're passionate about what you do, that enthusiasm spreads. It lifts the morale of your team, enhances your company's culture, and even positively impacts your clients or customers. You're creating a feast, not just a meal— every action you take in alignment with your authentic self nourishes not only your own life but also the lives of those around you. You invite others to the banquet, while enjoying your spot at the head of the table.

Spotting the ripple effect in your own life starts with awareness. Take a moment to reflect on a positive change you've made recently. Maybe you've started a daily gratitude practice, and now you notice that you're more appreciative of the small things. Has this newfound appreciation improved your relationships? Perhaps your partner feels more valued, or your friends notice your increased optimism. That's the ripple effect.

Another example could be setting boundaries at work to protect your personal time. At first, it might feel like a small step, but over time, you might notice that you're less stressed, more energized, and actually more productive during work hours. Your colleagues might even follow your lead, creating a healthier work environment for everyone.

When you invest in yourself, you're not just making your life better—you're contributing to a more positive, vibrant, and connected world. So, as you continue to put your money where your mouth is, remember that each action, no matter how small, has the power to create ripples that extend far beyond what you can see. Keep investing in yourself, and watch how the world around you transforms. Now, let's take a peek at some of the soul-centered ways you can put your money where your mouth is.

SOUL-CENTERED INVESTMENTS

Being soul-centered isn't the same as being self-centered. Prioritizing your well-being means you're better equipped to help others and contribute more meaningfully to the world. It's about creating a solid foundation from which you can operate effectively and authentically—and, of course, with more ease. Remember the airplane safety instructions: put on your oxygen mask first. Focusing on soul-centered investments ensures you have the energy and resources to thrive in all areas of your life. It's not selfish; it's essential.

EDUCATION AND SKILL BUILDING

Investing in education is more than just a résumé boost—it's a way to deepen your connection with your passions. It's easy to think of education as something formal, like a degree program or a certification course. And yes, those are valuable investments. But what about the workshops, retreats, and online classes that speak directly to your soul? What about learning that isn't just about earning more money but about feeding your curiosity and expanding your understanding of the world?

For example, investing in a creative writing course might not seem like a direct path to success, but if writing is what lights you up, that course is an investment in your joy and fulfillment. Or perhaps you've always wanted to learn a new language—doing so could open up new cultures, travel opportunities, and ways of thinking that enrich your life in unexpected ways. When you invest in learning that aligns with your passions, you're not just adding another skill to your toolkit—you're expanding your capacity to live a life that feels true to you.

SELF-CARE

"Self-care" has become a bit of a buzzword, often reduced to spa days and skin-care routines. While those things are wonderful, real self-care goes deeper. It's about creating practices that nourish your mind, body, and soul on a regular basis. This might mean setting aside time each day for meditation, journaling, or simply sitting quietly with your thoughts. It might mean putting your energy into simple pleasures like baking, walks with a loved one, or saying yes to opportunities you'd otherwise deny yourself. Self-care could be turning off social media, taking a trip alone, or making a change to your physical appearance. It could mean seeking out therapy or coaching to work through past traumas or to gain clarity on your current path.

For me, self-care has also meant learning when to say no. It's about recognizing when my energy reserves are low and giving myself permission to rest, even if the world around me is buzzing with activity. It's about making sure I'm not just running on fumes but instead filling my tank with the things that truly restore me—whether that's spending time in nature, ecstatic dancing, hosting retreats, driving with the windows down, or binge-watching my favorite series for the eleventh time. When you prioritize self-care, you ensure that you have the energy and resilience to pursue your goals and dreams without burning out or projecting unprocessed emotions.

PROFESSIONALS AND FINANCES

Investing in yourself often requires enlisting the help of professionals—those who can offer guidance, expertise, and support that you might not be able to provide for yourself. Working with professionals like therapists, coaches, mentors, or financial advisors is a crucial aspect of self-investment. These individuals bring an outside perspective, helping you to see things clearly and navigate challenges more effectively. They act as catalysts for your growth, offering tools and insights that can accelerate your journey toward a more fulfilled and aligned life.

It's not just about spending money—it's about making conscious choices regarding where to allocate your resources to best support your goals. Whether it's paying for a course to develop a new skill, hiring a personal trainer to enhance your physical health, or working with a therapist to address emotional challenges, these investments pay dividends in the form of a more balanced and fulfilling life. Money, in this context, becomes a tool for empowerment. It allows you to access the resources and support systems that enable you to grow and thrive. However, it's important to approach these investments with discernment. Not every opportunity or service will be the right fit for you, and it's essential to ensure that your financial investments align with your deeper values and needs. When you invest financially in your growth, you make a statement that you value yourself and your future. It's an act of self-respect, acknowledging that you're worth the time, money, and effort it takes to become the best version of yourself. This kind of investment often leads to a ripple effect, where the benefits extend beyond the initial purchase or service, influencing other areas of your life and opening up new opportunities for success and fulfillment.

BANKING ON MYSELF

When I was in college, I thought I had everything figured out. I got into the school that everyone said was "right"— you know, the one that society approves of, not the art school that secretly captured my heart. I was living on my own, feeling like the epitome of cool, fun, and interesting. But underneath it all, I was deeply depressed, and my vision of life felt like a smudged lens. I had invested in all these choices that promised a linear, successful path and a foundation for happiness, thinking it would fill the void. But instead, I found myself spiraling into a massive breakdown on the stairs of my first apartment.

If I didn't know who I was at my core—buried under layers of societal expectations and self-imposed bullshit—how was I ever going to figure out what I truly wanted? So, I did something radical: I broke down to my mom and I asked for help. I poured my heart out to her, admitting that

I felt completely lost and didn't have a clue who I really was. She helped me find a therapist who would become a game changer in my life. From our very first session, Dr. C finally saw me for who I was, not just the persona I'd been projecting. Dr. C had this uncanny ability to speak to the parts of me I couldn't access on my own.

It was in those sessions with Dr. C that I started to learn what authenticity really meant. It wasn't some buzzword; it was the key to unlocking everything that had been holding me back. But let me tell you: peeling off those layers of bullshit was no easy feat. It took years of deep work, of facing the parts of myself I'd been avoiding, and of letting go of what wasn't serving me.

Week after week, Dr. C guided me through situations with questions that forced me to really dig in and process my life. The conversations weren't just about what I wanted; they were about giving myself permission to want what I wanted and to be okay with letting go of the rest. Authenticity became the North Star of our sessions, and through this work, I learned acceptance—acceptance of myself, my choices, my desires, and my needs.

This relationship with Dr. C became one of the most pivotal in my life because it was in that room that I learned the pillars of this book: acceptance and authenticity. I invested in myself by investing in a resource that gave me deeper access to who I truly was. And that investment changed everything. It didn't just shift my worldview; it set me on a path that I'm incredibly proud to walk today.

Years later, I became a counselor myself and eventually a coach. I carry those moments of self-investment with me, understanding that if I could be a part of someone's journey the way Dr. C was a part of mine, my life would have profound meaning. I realized that helping others see they're worth investing in—because you are—is one of the most important things I can do.

Investing in yourself is the greatest asset you have. And as you stand on the brink of discovering your own path, let this be your reminder: you are worth every ounce of effort, every dollar, every moment of time you invest in yourself. Trust me, all these investments pay dividends in ways you can't even begin to imagine.

Now that you've started to see the value of self-investment, let's turn our attention to what you're investing in. Our next stop is the body's role in cultivating ease—how it responds to stress, how it guides you, and how it can become a sanctuary of ease.

CHAPTER 4

A BODY OF WORK

"The body is a funny piece of meat. How it inflates and deflates in order to keep you alive. But how simple words can fill you up or pierce the air out of you."

—Elizabeth Acevedo,
Clap When You Land

"In order to change, people need to become aware of their sensations and the way that their bodies interact with the world around them. Physical self-awareness is the first step in releasing the tyranny of the past."

—Bessel van der Kolk, The Body Keeps the Score: Brain, Mind, and Body in the Healing of Trauma

INTRODUCTION TO THE BODY

Welcome to the first part of our triple threat of ease: the body. And yes, you're getting two quotes this time because the body is dynamic and multifaceted and deserves both a poetic nod and a practical grounding. I wanted to cover all the bases—after all, your body does too.

Now, before I let you believe I am in any way a fitness guru, let's get one thing straight: this chapter isn't about chasing some impossible fitness standard. Instead, we're here to explore how your physical self is the bedrock of your overall well-being. Because let's face it—if your body isn't on board, your mind and spirit aren't going to be winning any races either. Just like you wouldn't bake a cake without making sure the oven's preheated, you can't expect to live a life of ease without first getting your body in the right condition.

Your body is more than just a vessel; it's the foundation that holds everything else together. It's your home base, your grounding force, the thing that inflates and deflates to keep you alive every single day. Yet this complex system can be profoundly affected by the simplest things—words, thoughts, emotions. It's easy to overlook how much our bodies carry, both physically and emotionally, and how this weight can impact our ability to live authentically and with ease.

Ease is more than a mental or emotional state; it's a full-body experience. It's deeply intertwined with how we treat and respect our bodies. If your foundation is shaky, everything else—your mental clarity, your emotional stability, and even your spiritual connection—starts to wobble. So this chapter is all about strengthening that foundation, ensuring that you can live in physical alignment with who you truly are.

Your body is the starting point for everything else you want to achieve in life. It's the anchor that keeps you grounded and the engine that drives you forward. But it's also the place where you store tension, trauma, and all those little stressors that pile up day after day. As Bessel van der Kolk points out, physical self-awareness is the first step in releasing the tyranny of the past. It's about tuning in to your body, understanding how it interacts with the world around you, and using that awareness to cultivate a life of ease and authenticity.

So, as we explore how to nurture this "funny piece of meat" we call the body, remember that the goal is not just getting physically healthy; it's creating a space where ease and authenticity can flourish. The mind and body are not separate entities—they're dance partners in this whole life thing. How you treat one will inevitably affect the other.

HOW DO YOU TALK TO THE BODY?

Let's start with a simple question: How do you talk to your body? No, I don't mean whispering sweet nothings into your biceps (though if that works for you, I'm jealous). I'm talking about tuning in, listening, and responding to what your body needs. Think of it as a daily check-in, like catching up with an old friend.

The way we talk to our bodies is more powerful than we often realize. Our bodies hold on to trauma, stress, and emotions—literally keeping the score of our experiences, as van der Kolk so eloquently points out. **Life Lesson:** If we continually criticize or ignore our bodies, we're reinforcing negative patterns that can make life harder. Imagine trying to build a house on a shaky foundation—it just doesn't work. But when we speak kindly to our bodies, acknowledging their strength, resilience, and capacity for healing, we create a stable foundation that supports ease and well-being.

It's important to remember that our bodies listen to everything we say, whether it's a mental critique about how we look in the mirror or a dismissive thought about how tired we feel. Negative self-talk can perpetuate stress and tension, making it difficult to access a state of ease. On the flip side, speaking positively to our bodies can help us release stored trauma, promote healing, and ultimately make life feel lighter and more manageable.

Before we dive into any physical exercises or routines, it's crucial to start with how we talk to and about our bodies. Ask yourself: *Is my inner dialogue making my life easier or harder? Are the things I say to myself reinforcing tension and negativity, or are they creating space for healing and ease?*

A great way to ease into this conversation with your body is with a body-scan exercise. This is a simple yet powerful tool that helps you tune in to your body, identify areas of tension, and communicate with yourself in a way that's rooted in kindness and awareness. Here's how you can do it.

STEP 1: FiND A COMFORTABLE PoSiTiON

→ Sit or lie down in a comfortable position. Close your eyes and take a few deep breaths, allowing your body to relax.

→ **Internal Dialogue:** *I'm giving myself permission to take this time to connect with my body. I deserve to feel at ease.*

STEP 2: START AT THE TOP

→ Begin by focusing on the top of your head, and slowly work your way around your skull. Notice any sensations, tension, or areas that feel relaxed.

→ The crown chakra (space above your head)

represents your connection to the divine and your higher self.

→ **Internal Dialogue:** *How does my head feel? Is there tension in my forehead or scalp? Can I let it go? I open myself to clarity and spiritual connection.*

STEP 3: MOVE DOWN TO YOUR FACE

→ Shift your attention to your face, particularly the area between your eyebrows, your jaw, and any muscles that might be working overtime. Can you breathe into these spots and release any tension?

→ The third-eye chakra (between your eyebrows) governs intuition, imagination, and wisdom.

→ **Internal Dialogue:** *I tune in to my intuition and inner wisdom. I trust the insights that come to me. I let the stress of my day and worries go now.*

STEP 4: FOCUS ON YOUR THROAT

→ Next, bring your focus to your throat and notice any sensations of tension, shallow breathing, withholding of truth, oversharing, or fatigue.

→ The throat chakra (the neck) is associated with communication and self-expression.

→ **Internal Dialogue:** *I release any tension in my throat. I express myself clearly and truthfully. I am grateful for my truth.*

STEP 5: MOVE DOWN TO YOUR SHOULDERS AND ARMS

→ Notice how your shoulders and arms feel. Are they tight or relaxed? Are you holding tension here? Are your hands clenched or relaxed?

→ **Internal Dialogue:** *My shoulders carry a lot. I'm acknowledging that and letting them relax. My arms are strong, and I appreciate all they do for me.*

STEP 6: FOCUS ON YOUR CHEST AND HEART

→ Pay attention to your chest; notice your breathing and any sensations around your heart. How fast or slow is it beating? Does it feel contracted or expansive? Does it feel light or heavy? Are you able to identify where your feelings are being activated, or are you stuck in your head?

→ The heart chakra is all about love, compassion, and emotional balance.

→ **Internal Dialogue:** *I open my heart to love and compassion for myself and others. I'm breathing deeply, filling my lungs with ease. My heart is strong and beats with purpose.*

STEP 7: SCAN YOUR STOMACH, NAVEL, AND LOWER BACK

→ Notice how your stomach and lower back feel. Are there knots of tension or areas of discomfort? Is there a deeper knowing you're processing or ignoring? Do you trust your gut?

→ The solar-plexus chakra (area above the navel) represents personal power, confidence, and self-esteem.

→ **Internal Dialogue:** *I release any stress I'm holding in my stomach. My body is capable of digesting and processing all that life gives me. I embrace my personal power and confidence. I release any knots of tension and stand strong in who I am.*

→ Move your attention to the area below your navel and notice any sensations of temperature or pressure.

→ The sacral chakra (area below the navel) is connected to creativity, pleasure, and emotional well-being.

→ **Internal Dialogue:** *I honor my creativity and allow myself to experience joy and pleasure. I release any emotional blocks here.*

STEP 8: MOVE DOWN TO YOUR HIPS AND LEGS

→ Focus on your hips, thighs, and knees. Are they tense or relaxed? Do they feel tight or loose? Are you feeling lubricated or hearing cracks? How much stress is being stored in these areas?

→ The root chakra (the base of your spine) represents your foundation, security, and grounding.

→ **Internal Dialogue:** *My hips support me in all that I do. I let go of any tightness here. My legs are strong*

*and carry me forward with ease. I am grounded,
stable, and secure.*

STEP 9: FINISH WITH YOUR FEET

→ Finally, focus on your feet. Notice any sensations, areas of tension, or lack of care. Our feet have pressure points connected to almost every other part of the body, so notice if any point on your foot is carrying a specific feeling. Do you feel grounded when you stand? Do you compensate in other body parts? Do your feet ever touch the earth? How do you carry yourself?

→ **Internal Dialogue:** *My feet ground me. They support me in every step I take. I appreciate the balance they provide. My feet connect me to the earth, and I move forward with confidence.*

STEP 10: REFLECT

→ Take a moment to reflect on how your body feels after the scan. Notice any areas that felt particularly tense or relaxed.

→ **Internal Dialogue:** *I've checked in with my body, and I'm grateful for its signals. I commit to listening and responding with kindness.*

By practicing this body scan regularly, you start to cultivate a more positive and attentive relationship with your body. It's about creating a dialogue that supports ease, healing, and authenticity—laying the groundwork for a life that feels not just manageable but genuinely fulfilling.

This body scan is more than just a relaxation exercise—it's a way to connect with yourself on a deeper level. When you regularly check in with your body, you start to notice patterns and signals that you might have ignored before. This awareness is the first step in breaking the cycle of negative self-talk and creating a more compassionate relationship with your physical self.

BREATHE AND BE

Let's talk about something we do all day, every day, without thinking: we breathe. (And yes, we blink too, but we'll stick to breathing for now—though if you're blinking right now, congrats, you're nailing that one as well.) Breathing is so automatic that we often forget how powerful it can be, especially when it comes to creating ease in our lives.

Life Lesson: Not all breathing is created equal. When we're stressed, our breathing tends to get shallow and rapid, barely filling our lungs. Some of us even hold our breath without realizing it, especially during moments of tension—like when we're trying to get through a tough conversation or waiting for the results of that all-important email. This kind of breathing actually signals to your body that it should stay in a state of stress, keeping your nervous system on high alert.

But here's where the magic happens: deep, diaphragmatic breathing (the kind that fills your belly and expands your lungs) can flip the script entirely. This type of breathing encourages your body to relax, activating your parasympathetic nervous system (remember her?!), which is responsible for calming you down and promoting a state of ease. It's like sending a message to your brain that says, *Hey, it's all good. We've got this.*

Breathing is more than just an oxygen delivery system. It's a tool that can help regulate your emotions, reduce anxiety, and bring your body back to a state of balance. When you breathe deeply and fill your lungs, you're nourishing your body with life-sustaining energy and giving your mind a chance to reset. Deep breathing can lower your heart rate, reduce your blood pressure, and even improve your digestion. It's like a built-in stress-relief button that you can press anytime, anywhere. By practicing deep breathing regularly, you train your body to stay calm under pressure. It becomes easier to manage stress, make clear decisions, and stay present in the moment. Plus, it's a simple, free way to care for yourself—no fancy equipment or gym membership required.

HOW TO BREATHE DEEPLY

In case you're holding your breath right now (you're not alone—I'm guilty of this habit too), let's walk through a simple deep-breathing exercise that you can do anytime you need to create a moment of ease. This is the 4-7-8 breathing technique, or the box breath, which is especially effective for calming the mind and body.

1. **Find a Comfortable Position:** Sit or lie down in a comfortable position. Close your eyes if that helps you focus.

2. **Inhale:** Take a slow, deep breath in through your nose for a count of four. As you inhale, focus on filling your belly with air, allowing it to rise as your lungs expand.

3. **Hold:** Gently hold your breath for a count of seven. This pause helps to oxygenate your blood and gives your body a moment to adjust.

4. **Exhale:** Slowly exhale through your nose for a count of eight. As you do, imagine letting go of any tension or stress in your body. Feel your shoulders drop, your jaw unclench, and your mind quiet.

5. **Repeat:** Continue this cycle for four to eight rounds or until you feel a sense of calm washing over you.

This exercise is like hitting the reset button on your nervous system. It's a quick way to bring yourself back to a state of ease, whether you're in the middle of a hectic workday or winding down for the evening.

When you make deep breathing a regular part of your routine, you both create moments of calm in the present and build resilience for the future. Over time, you'll notice that it becomes easier to manage stress, stay focused, and maintain your sense of inner peace, even in challenging situations. It's like building muscle—the more you practice, the stronger your ability to stay calm and collected becomes.

So, the next time you're feeling overwhelmed, remember that you have the power to shift your state with just a few deep breaths. And while you're at it, maybe take a moment to blink and refocus your vision on what truly matters. Because, as it turns out, taking care of your body isn't just about exercise or diet—it's about the small, intentional actions that add up to a life of ease and authenticity.

RITUALS AND ROUTINES

Just like a car needs regular maintenance to keep it running smoothly, your body and mind thrive on consistency. But here's the thing: it's not enough to slap together any old routine and call it a day. The magic lies in creating rituals and routines tailored to your specific needs and goals, helping you operate at your best. Think of your daily routine as a custom-built, well-oiled machine designed to keep you in top form. Routines are more than just a series of repetitive tasks; they're a framework that provides stability and reduces decision fatigue. When you have a routine in place, you don't have to waste mental energy figuring out what to do next—you can focus that energy on more important things. Establishing a routine can also help signal to your brain that it's time to shift gears, whether you're waking up, winding down, or preparing to tackle a big project.

COOKING UP YOUR ROUTINE: THE RECIPE

Creating a routine is like crafting the perfect recipe (the path to ease is basically a cookbook, guys)—it's all about knowing your ingredients, balancing flavors, and making sure the result is something you'll enjoy (and want to keep making). Here's how to whip up a routine that supports your well-being, authenticity, and life getting to be easy:

1. **Gather Your Ingredients (Identify Your Goals)**
   Start by asking yourself what you want to achieve with your routine. Are you looking to boost your energy levels, improve focus, reduce stress, or maybe all of the above? Knowing your goals is like knowing which dish you want to cook—it guides the rest of the process and helps you choose the right "ingredients" (activities) to include.

2. **Start with a Pinch (Start Small)**
   Just like you wouldn't throw a whole jar of spice into your dish, don't overwhelm yourself by trying to overhaul your entire day at once. Begin with one

or two key habits that align with your goals. For example, if you want to reduce stress, start with a morning meditation or a few minutes of deep breathing. A little seasoning goes a long way.

3. Stir Constantly (Be Consistent)
Consistency is key to getting those flavors to meld perfectly. Choose a time of day when you're most likely to stick with your new habits, and commit to doing them at the same time each day. This helps "cook" the habit into your daily life, making it easier to maintain over time.

4. Taste and Tweak (Evaluate and Adjust)
While consistency is important, even the best recipes need a little tweaking now and then. Pay attention to how your body and mind respond to your routine. Periodically take stock of what's working and what's not, and make adjustments as needed. This flexibility ensures that your routine remains effective and aligned with your current priorities, just as you'd adjust seasoning to suit your taste. You might alternate between dance (yoga is great, but dancing is a vibe), journaling (or sending yourself voice memos with your thoughts or observations), and creative projects (the ideas that feel good and nurturing) to keep your routine fresh and engaging. Variety is the spice of life, after all.

By following this "recipe," you'll create a routine that not only supports your goals but also becomes something you genuinely look forward to each day. Over time, your body will adapt to this routine, and you'll become more attuned to when something feels off or what might be adding unnecessary stress to your life. Establishing a routine is like training a puppy—it gives your body purpose and exercises its functions, helping it to run smoothly. So, start cooking, and enjoy the process of fine-tuning your daily "dish" to perfection!

EXAMPLE ROUTINE: MORNING TUNE-UP

To put this approach into practice, here's an example of a morning routine that hits all the right notes.

→ **Hydration:** Start your day with a glass of water to kick-start your metabolism and rehydrate your body after sleep.

→ **Nutrition:** Fuel up with a balanced breakfast that includes protein, healthy fats, and complex carbs to keep your energy levels steady.

→ **Movement:** Stretch or do a short workout to wake up your muscles and get your blood flowing.

→ **Mindfulness:** Spend a few minutes in meditation, deep breathing, or journaling to set a positive tone for the day.

→ **Plan:** Take a moment to review your goals for the day, prioritizing tasks that align with your overall objectives.

INTUITIVE EATING: LISTEN TO YOUR GUT (LITERALLY)

Intuitive eating is all about tuning in to your body's natural signals—hunger, fullness, and even cravings—and making food choices that nourish both your body and your soul. It's not about following strict diets, counting calories, or depriving yourself of the foods you love. Instead, we can create a relationship with food that feels balanced, enjoyable, and sustainable. When you pay attention to what your body is truly asking for, you'll find that you naturally gravitate toward foods that make you feel good, both physically and emotionally. Intuitive eating finds that sweet spot—a place where you can enjoy food without guilt, honor your body's needs, and make choices that feel good in the long run. It's a practice that encourages mindfulness and self-compassion, allowing you to trust your body and its wisdom. Intuitive eating takes away the pressure to conform to external standards and instead focuses on what feels right for you. This practice aligns with the idea that life doesn't have to be a constant struggle; it can be easier when you trust yourself and listen to your body.

THE ART OF RESTING EASY

Sleep isn't just a luxury; it's a foundational ingredient in your recipe for a life of ease—like the perfect amount of butter in a dish. Without it, everything crumbles. We often treat sleep like an afterthought, surviving on caffeine and willpower, but that's not sustainable. Quality sleep is the unsung hero, quietly working behind the scenes to keep you sharp and ready to handle life's challenges. Creating a bedtime ritual can help you wind down and recharge, setting the stage for true rest. But let's distinguish between rest and *rich* rest. Rich rest isn't mindless scrolling or Netflix bingeing; it's about centering yourself, calming your nervous system, and embracing stillness— whether through a nap, a bath, or sitting quietly in nature. Remember this saying: "Tension is who you think you should be. Relaxation is who you are." By cultivating rich rest, you're not just surviving; you're giving yourself the space to truly thrive. You're more in tune with your authentic self, better equipped to make decisions that align with your values, and able to handle challenges with grace.

Sleep is one of the most crucial but often overlooked forms of self-care. Skimping on it pushes us into overdrive, disconnecting us from our true selves and making life harder. Prioritizing sleep is essential to maintaining your sense of self and keeping life manageable. It's not just about resting your head—it's about giving yourself permission to recharge and show up as your best self. So, next time you're tempted to stay up late, remember: rich rest makes everything easier. As Leonardo da Vinci said, "A well-spent day brings happy sleep." And in the words of Beyoncé, "Having peace, happiness, and healthiness is my definition of beauty. And you can't have any of that without sleep." Now, go get some rest—you've earned it.

WHAT IS PLEASURE TO YOU?

Let's take a deeper dive into the concept of pleasure and its impact on our lives. We're not just talking about the simple joys, like enjoying a good meal or watching your favorite TV show (though I could live off my guilty-pleasure series and be perfectly content). We're talking about a deeper, more profound connection to pleasure that can transform the way you live, think, and feel. Pleasure, in its truest form, is an essential part of our physical and psychological well-being. I've included it in this chapter because I believe that fully understanding its psychological benefits requires physical immersion. Pleasure goes beyond indulgence to creating a life that feels good from the inside out.

At its core, pleasure is a complex neurological response. When we engage in activities that bring us joy, our brain releases dopamine, a neurotransmitter that reinforces those behaviors by creating a sense of reward. This release of dopamine then makes us want to repeat pleasurable activities, driving us to seek out experiences that satisfy us. But here's the **Life Lesson:** pleasure isn't just about chasing fleeting moments of happiness—it's about cultivating a sustainable sense of well-being that permeates every aspect of our lives. Pleasure is intricately linked to our sense of purpose and fulfillment. Engaging in activities that bring us deep joy makes us feel good in the moment, but the effect also goes deeper than that, aligning our actions with our true selves and our core values. This alignment fosters a sense of authenticity; the pleasure we experience becomes a reflection of our true desires and not just external expectations.

When we consistently engage in activities that resonate with us on a deeper level, we create a positive feedback loop. The more we experience authentic pleasure, the more we understand who we are, what we truly value, and what we're capable of achieving. This deeper understanding allows us to live more intentionally, making choices that align with our purpose and bring lasting fulfillment. Pleasure helps to reduce stress, enhance our resilience, and improve our overall mental health. It acts as a buffer against the pressures of life, allowing us to navigate challenges with greater ease. By prioritizing pleasure, we're not being self-indulgent but rather engaging in a form of self-*care* that supports our overall well-being.

PLEASURE PRACTICES

Now, let's dive into the ingredients of pleasure—because, like any good recipe, the magic lies in balance, variety, and maybe a sprinkle of humor to keep things interesting. If you're wondering where to start or what pleasure truly means to you, remember that pleasure is a vast spectrum. There are infinite ways to cultivate and experience joy, happiness, fulfillment, and even enlightenment. But if you're looking for a few touchstones to get you started, below are some key ingredients.

→ **Mindful Indulgence:** Immerse yourself fully in the activities that bring you joy, but do so with intention. For instance, if you're enjoying a piece of dark chocolate, let it melt slowly on your tongue, appreciating the complexity of flavors. Opt for a high-quality, rich cacao bar that not only satisfies your sweet tooth but also supports your well-being. (*Pro tip*: This is your chance to make eating chocolate feel like a spiritual experience. No judgment if you feel like whispering sweet nothings to your dessert before devouring it.) Or, if nature calls to you, take a walk in the woods, but don't just stroll—tune in to the rustling leaves, the scent of pine, and the feel of the earth beneath your feet.

→ **Creative Expression:** Dive into creative outlets that allow you to express your true self. This isn't about creating a gallery-worthy piece of art; it's about the joy of the process. For example, if you're into painting, don't worry about perfecting every brushstroke. Instead, let the colors flow freely and allow your emotions to guide your hand. Writing can be another powerful outlet—whether it's journaling your thoughts, crafting a poem, or starting that novel you've always dreamed of. Dance like no one's watching, literally! Whether it's full-on choreography or just moving to the beat in your living room, let your body express itself. And if music is your thing, pick up an instrument—even if you're only strumming a few chords on a guitar or tinkering with the piano keys, let the sound be your release. (And remember: finger painting and adult coloring books are totally acceptable forms of creative expression, no matter your age. It's about the joy, not the result.)

→ **Physical Pleasure:** This encompasses so much more than just the obvious (though I'll get to that in a moment). It's about treating your body like the temple it is. Start with a deep stretch in the morning—reach for the sky, feel your muscles lengthen, and notice how it grounds you for the day ahead. Or sink into a warm bath at the end of a long day, letting the water soothe your muscles and calm your mind. Feel the warmth of the sun on your skin—take a moment to bask in it, allowing the rays to recharge your energy. (Yes, lying in the sun like a lizard totally counts as self-care. Just remember the sunscreen!) Don't underestimate the power of touch either. Whether it's through a hug from a loved one, the sensation of your favorite blanket, or even a self-massage, these moments of physical pleasure remind you to be present in your body.

→ **Sexual Pleasure:** This goes beyond physical satisfaction—it's about deep connection and self-discovery. Engage your senses and explore what truly brings you joy, whether solo or with a partner. Effective communication is key—express your desires, set boundaries, and explore fantasies together. This isn't just about the destination; it's about enjoying the journey of pleasure and connection. By embracing sexual pleasure, you align more deeply with your authentic self, enhancing ease and fulfillment in all areas of your life. (So light those candles, put on that playlist, and remember—pleasure is your birthright, and it's okay to fully embrace it in all its forms.)

→ **Connection:** Building and nurturing meaningful relationships can be one of the deepest sources of pleasure. Connection means not just being around people but truly engaging with them. Plan a dinner with friends where phones are banned from the table, and see how the conversation flows when everyone is fully present. Share a heartfelt conversation with a loved one, listening more than you speak. (*Pro tip:* Rediscover the art of eye contact—it's amazing how good it feels to look through the window of someone's soul.) Spend quality time with those who lift you up, whether it's through laughter, shared activities, or simply being in each other's company. The memories you create through these connections represent the foundation of a life well lived.

→ **Exploration:** Don't be afraid to step outside your comfort zone and try something new. This could be as adventurous as traveling to a new country or as simple as taking up a hobby you've never tried before. Maybe it's cooking a dish from a cuisine you've never tasted or signing up for a pottery class just to see what happens when you get your hands dirty. Explore the unknown and you might discover unexpected sources of joy. Ever been to a poetry slam or tried indoor rock climbing? How about axe throwing or paddleboarding? These experiences not only broaden your horizons but also help you learn more about yourself and what you truly enjoy. (And who knows? Maybe you'll find out you're an axe-throwing prodigy or the Bob Ross of pottery!)

SHEDONISM: MY PERMISSION SLIP FOR PLEASURE

Shedonism didn't just appear out of nowhere—it was born out of my personal journey and struggle with the concept of pleasure. Growing up, I was what you might call a hedonist. I loved indulging in the pleasures of life—good food, fun experiences, deep connections (and yes, the sex, drugs, and rock-and-roll types of tendencies—sorry, Mom and Dad). But society often judges those who embrace pleasure openly, especially women. We're taught to be cautious, to hold back, to not be too much. In many ways, I saw pleasure as something to be earned or something that could easily slip into indulgence and excess.

I spent years wrestling with the notion that something was inherently wrong with me for simply following what felt right and interesting to me. While my peers were often cautious or even judgmental of my choices, I found myself caught between feeling isolated and shameful on the one hand and empowered and wiser on the other. I wasn't always a saint, but I was never much of a sinner either— just someone who chose to explore life fully. Still, it was hard not to feel like an outlier, especially when those same people who judged me would later come to me for advice, perspective, or just a nonjudgmental ear. I was the friend you could call to talk about anything, and I never judged— because I didn't see the point. Life, to me, was about experimenting and discovering what makes us feel alive.

In college, I minored in philosophy, and that's where I first encountered the concept of hedonism. Historically, it's painted in a pretty bad light, often reduced to a life of reckless indulgence and selfish pursuits. I was living out a version of that philosophy for myself, seeking pleasure as a way to understand life more deeply—and I was met with resistance, judgment, and a sense of otherness from those around me. I found myself constantly defending my choices, holding back smirks when people who once judged me started trying the very things they had criticized.

Eventually, I got fed up with having to explain myself. I realized there was something deeper and more divine than just the surface-level indulgence that people associated with hedonism. There was an opportunity for reclamation—a chance to rewrite the narrative around pleasure. I wanted to reclaim that narrative. I wanted to give myself and others permission to seek and enjoy pleasure without guilt or shame. And that's how Shedonism was born as a philosophy that destigmatizes personal fulfillment and pleasure-seeking. Shedonism isn't just about indulging; it's about being intentional with your pleasure, aligning it with your values, and allowing it to be a source of growth and self-discovery. It's a reclamation of feeling good for the highest good of all, a life of ease and purpose—and it's a reminder that life is meant to be lived fully, without the constraints of outdated moral judgments.

Shedonism has become the cornerstone of my coaching practice because it's a way of living that honors the whole self—mind, body, and spirit. It's about giving yourself the freedom to explore what brings you joy and fulfillment and then integrating those experiences into your daily life. This approach is rooted in divine feminine compassion, but it doesn't exclude anyone. It's about embracing pleasure in a way that is balanced, intentional, and aligned with your true self. For example, society often criticizes indulgences like enjoying a decadent dessert, taking a lazy afternoon nap, or even exploring sexual pleasure as being frivolous or self-indulgent. However, Shedonism reframes these acts as essential components of a fulfilling life. Instead of seeing that dessert as a "guilty pleasure," I see it as an opportunity to savor the moment, to experience joy and gratitude for the simple pleasures of life. That lazy nap? It's a way to honor your body's need for rest and rejuvenation, a form of self-care that allows you to show up as your best self. As for sexual pleasure, it's not just a physical act; it's a profound expression of connection, intimacy, and self-love. (See the Reframe to Reclaim method in action?!)

Shedonism isn't about excess or recklessness; it's about giving yourself permission to experience pleasure in all its forms without the weight of guilt or societal judgment. It's about reclaiming the parts of yourself that have been suppressed or shamed and allowing them to shine brightly. In the end, Shedonism reminds us that life is meant to be lived fully and authentically. It's about rewriting the rules and creating a life that is rich with purpose, pleasure, and meaning. So go ahead—embrace your inner shedonist, and do it with intention and alignment. After all, pleasure isn't the enemy; it's part of your clarity compass—a tool for tuning in to your inner guidance system that helps you align with your true self. (I'll say more about this in chapter 7.)

And if anyone asks why you're so content, so full of life and joy, just tell them you've decided to live by a new mantra: **Pleasure is my permission slip to live authentically, and I'm not apologizing for it.**

A BODY OF WORK

Through my journey with Shedonism, I've come to see my life as a body of work—a living, breathing artistry where every choice, every pleasure, and every challenge contributes to the masterpiece that is my existence. I've pushed my body to its limits and danced on the edge of my comfort zone. I've embraced pleasure in all its forms, not as a mere indulgence but as a gateway to deeper self-understanding. Through this process, I've learned who I am, what I truly desire, and what I'm capable of achieving. This isn't just about satisfying cravings or seeking momentary thrills; it's about living with intention, about curating a life that feels as good on the inside as it looks on the outside.

Our bodies hold our memories, our joys, and our traumas. They reflect the care—or neglect—we've given them, and they respond in kind. The way we move, breathe, and nourish ourselves directly influences the quality of our lives. When we honor our bodies as integral to our journey, we create a foundation that supports not just our physical health but also our mental clarity, emotional balance, and spiritual growth. Our bodies are indeed funny pieces of meat, as Elizabeth Acevedo so aptly put it. They inflate and deflate to keep us alive, but they also respond profoundly to the words we speak and the care we give them. Just as simple words can fill us up or deflate us, the way we treat our bodies—whether with kindness or neglect—shapes our experience of life. They're more than just the sum of their parts—they're the very foundation of our journey, capable of holding both our joy and our pain, and deserving of our deepest care.

Life is, in many ways, a body of work—each day, each moment, is a brushstroke on the canvas of our existence. And like any masterpiece, it's made possible through the body that carries us, the vessel through which we experience, express, and engage with the world. Our bodies are more than just vehicles for getting from point A to point B; they are the very mediums through which we create our lives. Every decision we make, every experience we seek, and every challenge we overcome is filtered through our physical selves.

Your body is your foundation, your anchor in this world. How you treat it—how you nourish it, move it, and yes, even how you speak to it—directly impacts how you experience life. When you allow yourself the freedom to seek pleasure, explore boundaries, and invest in practices that make you feel good, you're not just making life easier; you're enriching it. So, as you move forward, ask yourself:

What masterpiece is my body crafting? And as we shift gears to the mind, remember: while the brain stirs up the recipe for ease, your body is the bowl that holds it all together.

CHAPTER 5

DON'T PSYCH
YOURSELF OUT

*"To find out what is truly individual
in ourselves, profound reflection is
needed, and suddenly we realize how
uncommonly difficult the discovery of
individuality is."*

—C.G. Jung

PSYCH! IT GETS TO BE EASY!

As you've journeyed through the first few chapters, you've started to unravel the layers that make up your identity—your desires, your blocks, your values. And maybe you've even rediscovered something about your body and the impact it has on letting life be easy. Now, we have reached a critical juncture in this journey: understanding the psychological forces at play beneath the surface. It's here that we explore not just what drives you but how your mind can either propel you forward or hold you back. C.G. Jung's observation about the difficulty of discovering individuality rings true, especially when our brains are wired to protect us, often in ways that keep us from our most authentic selves.

Let's be real—when you hear the word "psychology," your first thought might be, *Oh no, here comes the boring stuff.* (Trust me, sitting through lectures on neural pathways wasn't exactly a rager.) But understanding what's happening in your brain is like getting the cheat codes for life. The more you know about how your mind works, the better you can navigate through stress and find that sweet spot of ease we've been talking about.

This chapter will pull back the curtain on the psychological mechanisms that influence your day-to-day life. We'll explore how stress affects your brain, why certain situations trigger you more than others, and what happens when you find yourself either in a state of flow or stuck in a cycle of anxiety. By understanding these mechanisms, you'll gain insight into the barriers you face and the tools you can use to navigate them.

As we dive into the science behind ease and stress, keep Jung's words in mind: this journey is about discovering the unique workings of your mind and how you can harness that knowledge to live a life that feels more aligned with who you truly are.

THE STRESS RESPONSE: FIGHTING AGAINST THE CURRENT

Imagine this: you're swimming in the ocean, when suddenly, a rip current pulls you away from the shore. Your heart races, your breathing becomes shallow, and all you can think about is survival. That's your sympathetic nervous system (SNS) kicking in, also known as the fight-or-flight response. It's great for getting you out of immediate danger, like when a bear is chasing you (or, more realistically, when you're late for a meeting). But when this response gets activated over and over—say, by constant work deadlines or that never-ending to-do list—it's like swimming against the current all the time. Exhausting, right? When you're stressed, your body releases stress hormones like adrenaline and cortisol. That response is your body's way of saying, *Uh, hello, something important is happening! Pay attention!* But here's what no one tells you that we all learn the hard way: prolonged exposure to these hormones can start to mess with your mind, including the consequences below.

→ **Impaired Prefrontal Cortex Function:** Think of your prefrontal cortex as the CEO of your brain. It's in charge of decision-making, planning, and keeping you from doing something you'll regret later (like sending that angry email). But when you're stressed, the CEO starts taking long lunch breaks, leaving you struggling to make decisions and control your impulses.

→ **Enhanced Amygdala Activity:** Meanwhile, your amygdala—the brain's emotional fire alarm—is on high alert. This is why you might find yourself overreacting to minor annoyances, like when someone cuts in front of you in traffic. The offense is not that bad, but your brain is primed to see danger everywhere.

→ **Slower Hippocampus Processing:** Imagine your hippocampus—the part of your brain responsible for memory and learning—as your personal librarian. Normally, it's great at filing away all your experiences neatly so you can recall them when needed. But under stress, that librarian is running around frantically, dropping books, and misplacing files. This is why you might find yourself forgetting simple things, like where you put your keys, or missing important details in a conversation. Your brain is so busy dealing with the stress that it just can't keep everything organized.

Under stress, your brain loves to mess with you by distorting reality. Suddenly, small problems seem like insurmountable mountains. This is known as catastrophizing. You might also start seeing the world in black and white; either everything is perfect or it's a total disaster. Sound familiar? These are classic cognitive distortions, and they can make life feel way harder than it needs to be.

THE RIPPLE EFFECT OF STRESS

We all handle stress differently, and I don't need to bombard you with statistics to explain how stress creeps into our lives every day, but...**Life Lesson:** If we don't take the time to really understand what stress is and how it's impacting us, it just becomes this background noise that we accept as part of life. No one really teaches us how to deal with it or find peace with it. When your brain is in overdrive, it's not just your thoughts that suffer—your entire life starts to feel like it's spiraling out of control. The impact of stress ripples outward, affecting your mind, your emotions, your behaviors, and even your relationships. You might find yourself snapping at friends or family over minor issues like someone leaving the cap off the toothpaste or not responding to a text quickly enough. These aren't just random outbursts; they're signs of a brain that's been pushed to its limits.

And it doesn't stop there. Persistent stress can cast a shadow over your mood, leaving you feeling anxious and sad for reasons you can't always pinpoint. It's like a cloud hanging over you that refuses to lift, making even the simplest tasks feel overwhelming. This emotional strain can lead you to retreat into yourself, withdrawing from social interactions and the activities you once enjoyed.

But perhaps one of the most insidious effects of chronic stress is the way it drives you toward maladaptive coping mechanisms. Instead of facing your problems head-on, you might find yourself overeating, using food as a comfort to numb the stress. Or maybe you turn to binge-watching Netflix, losing hours or even days in front of a screen to escape the reality of what's bothering you. In more extreme cases, some might turn to substances like alcohol or drugs as a form of self-medication, seeking temporary relief that only ends up creating more problems down the line.

These coping strategies might offer a brief reprieve, but they don't address the root of the problem. Instead, they often exacerbate the stress, creating a vicious cycle in which the very things you use to escape pull you deeper into the spiral. Stress, if left unchecked, has the potential to transform your life into a series of reactions rather than intentional actions, making it harder to connect with yourself and others in meaningful ways.

Understanding this ripple effect is crucial because it shows that stress isn't just a mental battle—it's a full-body, full-life experience. And the sooner you recognize the signs, the sooner you can start to find healthier, more sustainable ways to cope. Here's the good news: your brain isn't all doom and gloom. There's another state of being that we all strive for, whether we realize it or not: flow.

FLOW STATE AND EASE: FINDING THE SWEET SPOT

Flow is that magical state in which everything just clicks— you're fully absorbed in what you're doing, time seems to fly by, and the outside world fades into the background. It's like when you're so deep into a project that hours pass without you even noticing, or when you're playing a game, and all that matters is the next move. In these moments, you're not just working or playing; you're *in the zone.*

Neurologically speaking, flow is a fascinating phenomenon. It involves a reduction in activity in the prefrontal cortex— basically, your brain's overworked CEO finally gets a much-needed break. With the prefrontal cortex temporarily out of the picture, you're freed from the constant self-monitoring and second-guessing that can bog you down. Instead, you enter a state of focused relaxation, where your brain runs on autopilot in the best possible way.

In the flow state, your brain also gets a nice boost of dopamine—the feel-good chemical that keeps you motivated and engaged. It's like a natural high that makes the task at hand not just bearable but actually enjoyable. This is why athletes describe being in the zone during peak performance or why creatives can lose themselves in their work for hours on end. It's a state of ease where effort and enjoyment intersect.

Finding flow is more than losing yourself in work or play; it's about locating that sweet spot where challenge meets skill (your clarity compass points you in the direction of your sweet spot!). If the task is too easy, you get bored. If it's too hard, you get frustrated. But when it's just right, you're perfectly balanced between effort and reward. This balance makes flow a powerful and pleasurable experience.

But flow isn't just reserved for those peak moments of productivity or creativity. You can cultivate it in your everyday life by aligning your activities with your strengths and passions. Whether it's cooking, writing, or even having a deep conversation, finding flow can turn ordinary moments into something extraordinary. And the best part? The more you practice finding flow, the more easily you can slip into this state of ease and fulfillment.

THE FLOW-STATE FLAVORS

In the flow state, it's like your brain is cooking up the perfect recipe for a perfect event. Several key psychological and neurological ingredients come together, creating that unique experience of being in the zone:

1. **Hypofrontality**

   → **What It Is:** In flow, there's a temporary reduction in activity in the prefrontal cortex, the area of the brain responsible for higher cognitive functions like self-reflection, planning, and impulse control.

   → **Impact:** This reduction, known as "transient hypofrontality," allows you to bypass your inner critic and overthinking tendencies, leading to a sense of freedom and creativity. You're less likely to worry about failure or judgment, which can liberate you to perform at your best.

2. **Dopamine Release**

   → **What It Is:** Dopamine is a neurotransmitter associated with pleasure, reward, and motivation.

   → **Impact:** During flow, your brain releases dopamine,

which not only enhances focus and motivation but also creates a sense of enjoyment and satisfaction. This chemical boost reinforces the behavior, making you more likely to seek out and repeat activities that induce flow.

3. Altered Sense of Time

→ **What It Is:** A common experience in flow is the distortion of time; it seems either to fly by or to slow down.

→ **Impact:** This altered time perception occurs because your brain's focus shifts entirely to the task at hand, with less cognitive processing dedicated to tracking time. This directed attention helps you stay deeply immersed in the activity without the distraction of clock-watching.

4. Suppression of the Default Mode Network (DMN)

→ **What It Is:** The DMN is a network of brain regions that becomes active when your mind is at rest. It's typically associated with daydreaming, self-referential thinking, and rumination.

→ **Impact:** During flow, the DMN is suppressed, which helps reduce self-conscious thoughts and distractions. The result is a more immersive and present-focused experience in which your attention is fully engaged with the task.

5. Enhanced Pattern Recognition

→ **What It Is:** Your brain becomes more adept at recognizing patterns and making connections between different pieces of information.

→ **Impact:** This heightened ability to see connections allows for quicker decision-making and more creative problem-solving. You might find yourself intuitively knowing the next step or solution without needing to consciously think it through.

6. Increased Autotelic Experience

→ **What It Is:** The term "autotelic" comes from the Greek words "auto," meaning self, and "telos," meaning goal. An autotelic experience is one in which the activity itself is intrinsically rewarding.

→ **Impact:** In flow, the activity becomes its own reward, independent of external outcomes or recognition. This intrinsic motivation drives you to continue the activity purely for the joy of doing it.

7. Balanced Challenge-Skill Ratio

→ **What It Is:** Flow occurs when there's a perfect balance between the challenge of the task and your skill level.

→ **Impact:** If a task is too easy, you become bored; if it's too difficult, you become anxious. But when the challenge matches your abilities, it engages you fully without overwhelming you, creating the ideal conditions for flow.

Understanding these psychological and neurological elements of flow can help you identify activities that might lead to flow and create environments conducive to entering this state more frequently.

FINDING YOUR FLOW

Let's get you into that sweet spot where challenge and skill meet—your personal portal to the zone where time melts away and creativity takes the wheel. Here's how to find your groove and ride the wave of effortless focus and flow.

STEP 1: PICK YOUR PASSION

→ First things first: pick an activity you love. Think of something that sparks joy but still has a bit of a challenge. Maybe it's writing, painting, coding, or playing the piano. Whatever it is, make sure it's something that lights you up.

STEP 2: SLICE IT AND DICE IT

→ Now, break your task into bite-sized pieces. Like a chef slicing veggies for a perfect stir-fry, you want manageable chunks. Writing? Focus on just one section or brainstorming ideas. Playing music? Zero in on a tricky passage. Keep it simple and digestible.

STEP 3: TURN UP (OR DOWN) THE HEAT

→ Be real with yourself—are you a newbie, a seasoned pro, or somewhere in between? Knowing where you stand helps you dial in the challenge level. If it's too easy, crank up the heat—tighten your deadline, add a twist, or aim for a higher standard. If it's too tough, dial it back—simplify the task, give yourself more time, or grab a helping tool. The goal is to feel *engaged*, not overwhelmed.

STEP 4: SET A TARGET

→ Every chef needs a recipe, right? Set a clear, juicy goal for this session. Maybe you'll aim to write five hundred words in thirty minutes or master that tricky guitar riff in an hour. This specificity gives your brain a delicious target to focus on, which is the secret sauce for flow.

STEP 5: BLOCK THE NOISE

→ Time to create your flow-friendly zone. Turn off those pesky notifications, close those twenty-seven browser tabs, and let the world know you're off the grid. You want to create a little bubble where it's just you and your task—nothing else.

STEP 6: DO THE DAMN THING

→ Now for the fun part—get started! Immerse yourself fully in the task, and keep an eye on how you're feeling. Are you engaged, or is something off? If you're not hitting the zone, don't panic—adjust the challenge level and keep going.

STEP 7: REFLECT AND REFINE

→ Once you've wrapped up, take a moment to reflect. Did you feel that magical flow state, or were you struggling to stay engaged? What can you tweak for next time? Every adventure is a learning experience, and this reflection helps you fine-tune your path to flow.

By practicing this exercise, you're essentially training your brain to find and maintain balance, making it easier to slip into a flow state in various aspects of your life. Honing this ability not only boosts your productivity but also enhances your overall sense of fulfillment and well-being.

ACHIEVING EASE: THE CALM FOLLOWING THE STORM

Do you experience ease after a flow state, or do you experience ease during and because of a flow state? The answer is both. Ease is like the exhalation after a storm— the calm that settles once the intensity subsides. During a flow state, you're deeply immersed and focused, which creates a sense of ease because everything aligns naturally. Afterward, that ease lingers, bringing a sense of relaxation and balance. Flow and ease are intertwined; flow is the immersion, and ease is the tranquility that follows. It's that moment when the storm has passed, and the sun breaks through the clouds, casting a warm, comforting glow on everything around you. Remember the introduction of this book and the cliff you were standing on? You've let the trek up that mountain be easy, and ease now shines upon you.

Psychologically, achieving ease is crucial because it allows your brain and body to recover from the constant demands of life. When you're in a state of ease, your parasympathetic nervous system (PNS) takes center stage. The PNS is often called the "rest and digest" system because it counteracts the "fight or flight" response of the SNS. When the PNS is activated, your body slows down— it reduces your heart rate, decreases cortisol levels (those pesky stress hormones), and increases alpha brain waves. Alpha waves are associated with a calm and relaxed yet alert state of mind, akin to the feeling you get during a yoga session or a walk in nature.

But ease isn't just about relaxation in the present moment—it makes an imprint on your sense of the past, present, and future, influencing your entire life experience.

THE PSYCHOLOGICAL IMPACT OF TIME

When you cultivate ease, you allow your brain to process past experiences with a clearer, more compassionate perspective. Instead of replaying past mistakes or traumas with the harshness of hindsight, ease gives you the space to reinterpret these events with understanding and forgiveness. This doesn't mean forgetting the past but rather integrating it in a way that brings peace instead of turmoil. Over time, this practice can transform how you view your personal history, helping you to let go of guilt, shame, or regret and to embrace a more empowered narrative.

In the present, ease is your ally in making better decisions. When you approach life from a place of authenticity and calm, you're more likely to respond to situations with thoughtfulness rather than reacting out of stress or fear. This calmness enhances your executive functioning, allowing the prefrontal cortex (the part of your brain responsible for planning, decision-making, and moderating social behavior) to operate more effectively. As a result, you're more creative, better at problem-solving, and able to engage more fully with the people and tasks around you.

Ease helps you envision your future without the constraints of anxiety or the burden of unrealistic expectations. When you plan your future from a place of ease, you're more likely to set goals that align with your true desires and values rather than those dictated by societal pressures or fear of failure. Moreover, the psychological benefits of ease—such as lower stress levels, improved mental health, and better physical well-being—create a foundation for a more sustainable and fulfilling future.

And let's not forget the impact of ease on the generations to come. When you model a life of ease, you set a powerful example for those around you, whether it's your children, your family members, or the community. You show them that life doesn't have to be a constant struggle and that balance and well-being are achievable goals. This modeling can create a ripple effect, inspiring others to prioritize their mental health, embrace ease, and pass those values down to future generations. The practice of ease becomes a legacy, one that transcends your individual experience and contributes to a culture that values well-being over burnout.

Achieving ease isn't just about finding peace in the moment—it's about building a life on a foundation of calm, clarity, and authenticity. It's about making choices that align with your true self, leading to better outcomes not just for you but also for those around you, now and in the future.

FROM REFLECTION TO ACTION: THERAPY VS. COACHING

Now that we've delved into the psychological framework explaining what supports or disrupts ease—from the brain's wiring to the mind's patterns—it's time to consider how working with a professional can help. Understanding the science is one thing, but translating that into lasting change is another, which is where the support of a therapist or a coach comes into play. Whether you're looking to unpack the past or propel into the future, these guides can help you bridge the gap between knowing what's going on in your mind and actually achieving that state of ease over time.

Think of therapy as looking through a window into your past. It's about exploring how you got to where you are—sifting through emotions, understanding patterns and family history, and having that crucial conversation about your feelings. Therapy offers reflection and insight, focusing on understanding and processing the past, which is invaluable but can sometimes feel like there's always something to fix.

If therapy is peeking into the past, coaching is strapping on your sneakers and sprinting toward the future. Coaching is all about forward momentum—using what you've learned about yourself to make measurable, tangible changes now. Coaching helps you shift gears from processing to doing. It's collaborative, results-focused, and designed to shift you from awareness to action, with an emphasis on setting goals and having accountability. It's about moving beyond awareness and championing change through uniquely curated sessions tailored to the client's needs. It's less about *why* and more about *how* and *what's next*.

I made the leap from therapist to coach because I believe in the power of actionable change and embracing the connection that forms between two individuals who are cocreating personal changes. I love to listen, *and* I love getting to be a part of the process of doing something with what we discover about ourselves in those conversations. (Don't get me wrong; I am not saying one option is better than the other. Both have profoundly shaped my life, and I believe both are game changers! For me, coaching feels like ease.) Therapy has long been the go-to; it's well-known and accessible, and it often focuses on healing and resolving issues over time. Now, coaching is gaining recognition for its ability to drive actionable change in a tangible timeframe, and I am excited for coaching to find its way to those who would deeply benefit from its hands-on approach.

Both therapy and coaching are powerful tools for managing stress, achieving flow, and finding ease, but they serve different purposes depending on where you are in your journey. Therapy lays the foundation, helping you understand your roots, while coaching builds the structure for your future, focusing on growth, change, and action. So, if you're feeling like you've done the inner work and are ready to take the next step toward a more aligned, intentional life—coaching might be your jam. It's where I blend my personality and mindfulness techniques into a collaborative relationship that's all about you, your goals, and your future. No hard sell here, just an invitation: if you're ready to make lasting changes and understand yourself on a deeper level, coaching might just be the path you're looking for.

Now, let's keep this momentum going as we move out of the mind and into the soul. Because let's be real—we can't talk about living a full life without acknowledging the role of our inner selves, our connection to something greater, and how our spirit might have a hand in making things easier. So get cozy, set an intention for ease, and maybe light a candle as we slide into our spiritual inbox (it's probably full of messages that need your attention).

CHAPTER 6

PLUG INTO POWER

"Just as a candle cannot burn without fire, people* cannot live without a spiritual life."

—Buddha

*The original quote says men, but let's be more inclusive, shall we?

INTRODUCTION TO THE SPIRIT

I told you to light a candle, didn't I?! Welcome to the final installment of our "Triple Threat of Ease" series. We've journeyed through the body and the mind, and now it's time to tap into the soul—the core that fuels everything else. Now, I know quoting Buddha might seem like calling in the head honcho for this chapter, but trust me, this is the kind of wisdom we need to tap into when we're talking about something as essential as the spirit. Buddha nailed it. But let's break that wisdom down, because it's not just about lighting some incense and calling it a day.

When Buddha talks about fire, he's pointing to something deeper—the essence that fuels our existence, the spark that keeps us going even when life throws its hardest punches. Spirituality isn't a checkbox on a wellness list; it's about connecting to something bigger than ourselves, finding that inner light that makes everything else come into focus. Whether you call it the universe, a higher power, or simply your inner compass, this is the fire that guides you and keeps you grounded when the world feels chaotic.

And if the closest you've come to spirituality is laughing at the jokes in *The Good Place* (a work of televised art, I dare say) or saving bite-sized motivational quotes on Instagram, don't worry—I've got you. This chapter is about making spirituality approachable, digestible, and, most importantly, meaningful for you.

This chapter is called "Plug into Power" because it's about consciously taking steps to connect with a higher power and truly embody spiritual practices. Think of it like charging your phone—you wouldn't expect it to hold power if you never plugged it in, right? The same goes for your spirit. You have to intentionally plug into the source, recharge, and stay connected to keep your spiritual energy flowing and your inner light shining bright.

Plugging into power isn't just going through the motions of spirituality; it's about actively engaging with the practices that ground you, uplift you, and connect you to something greater than yourself. It's about embodying these practices in your daily life—whether that's through mindfulness, meditation, prayer, or simply taking the time to listen to your inner voice. When you make that connection, you're filling your spiritual battery to light up your entire life. You're giving yourself the energy and clarity to navigate challenges, the wisdom to make aligned decisions, and the peace to live authentically. In essence, you're illuminating yourself from the inside out, allowing your true self to shine through in everything you do.

Let's talk about the saying "The universe has your back." Gabby Bernstein might have coined it, but it's a sentiment that resonates with any of us who've ever felt like something bigger than ourselves is at play in our lives. It's that comforting belief that no matter how chaotic, uncertain, or downright confusing life gets, there's a higher power looking out for you. When you truly believe that the universe is on your side, you're more likely to take risks, trust your intuition, and let go of the need to control every little detail. If you're new to this idea, it might seem a bit out there. But think of it this way: If life is a grand adventure, wouldn't it be nice to know there's a guide who's been on this path before? Someone who knows the shortcuts, the scenic routes, and the best spots to stop and enjoy the view? That's what it means for the universe to have your back. It's about leaning into the idea that there's a force working in your favor.

Whether you're a seasoned woo-woo enthusiast who aligns your crystals under every full moon (if you aren't bathing your crystals in moonlight, what ARE you doing?!) or someone who thinks "manifesting" is just fancy talk for wishful thinking, the presence of spirit is undeniable. For the skeptics and cynics, I understand—talk of destiny, fate, and cosmic contracts can feel a bit abstract, especially if you're grounded in the tangible world. But these concepts have endured across cultures for a reason: they tap into something deeper in the human experience.

Instead of dismissing them outright, consider them one way to make sense of life's complexities. You don't have to fully buy in, but exploring these ideas might offer you a new perspective, a sense of order in the chaos, and a reminder that your choices matter. **Life Lesson:** Spirituality isn't just about chanting "om" or wearing flowy clothes (my authenticity was in full force the day I threw out my skinny jeans, though, just sayin'). Think of spirituality as the flame that keeps your favorite dish simmering on the stove. Without it, everything cools down, loses flavor, and eventually goes stale.

This chapter is your guide to exploring the spiritual dimension of ease. We're going to cover everything from mindfulness to manifesting, with some astrological detours along the way (because why not?). By the end of it, you'll not only have a better understanding of how to plug into your spiritual power but also some practical tools to keep that fire burning bright. We're about to dive into the enlightened soul's side of ease.

MINDFULNESS AND PRACTICING PRESENCE: BE HERE NOW

Mindfulness is like the spiritual equivalent of kale—it suddenly became *the* thing for anyone wanting to be healthy, even though most of us had no idea what it was before it became trendy, let alone how to work it into our daily lives. Now, everyone tosses the word "mindfulness" around (more than they toss a kale salad), but do we really understand why it's so important? Let's clear that up right now. Mindfulness isn't just a trendy buzzword; it's the bedrock of any spiritual practice. It's where you start to cultivate the kind of awareness that makes life feel a little less like a chaotic scramble and more like a well-orchestrated dance.

Why are we talking about mindfulness here, in the spirituality chapter? Because it's the gateway. It's the practice that unlocks the door to all the other spiritual concepts we'll explore—intuition, higher purpose, synchronicity—by bringing you into the present moment where all these experiences actually happen. Without mindfulness, spirituality can feel abstract, disconnected, or even overwhelming. With it, you're grounded, clear, and ready to interact with the spiritual side of life in a meaningful way.

Mindfulness cultivates presence and clarity—two qualities that are essential for connecting with your inner self and higher purpose. When you're mindful, you're fully engaged in the present moment, not lost in the regrets of the past or the worries of the future. This state of presence is where true spiritual connection begins.

One of the most accessible ways to practice mindfulness is through breathwork. It's a simple yet profound way to bring yourself back to the here and now. Start by taking a few deep breaths, really focusing on the sensation of the air entering and leaving your body. Feel how your chest rises and falls, how the air feels cooler on the inhalation and warmer on the exhalation. Notice how this seemingly mundane act of breathing becomes a powerful anchor, pulling you into the present moment. This is mindfulness in action—a way to shift your perspective from the chaos of the mind to the calm of the moment.

But let's go beyond the basics. Mindfulness isn't limited to breathwork; it's about cultivating a deep awareness of your thoughts, feelings, and surroundings in every aspect of your life. Below are a few ways to integrate mindfulness into your daily routine.

→ **Mindful Eating:** Instead of rushing through meals, take the time to really taste your food. Notice the flavors, textures, and even the sounds of your meal. This not only enhances your eating experience but also brings you fully into the moment, making the act of eating a meditative practice. (Wouldn't it be cool to be able to distinguish flavors, like, "Why yes, that is cardamom"?)

→ **Mindful Movement:** Whether it's yoga, walking, or just stretching, move your body with awareness. Pay attention to how your muscles feel, how your body shifts and balances, and how your breath coordinates with your movements. This attention turns even the simplest exercise into a practice of mindfulness. (And hey, who knew that touching your toes could feel like a spiritual awakening?)

→ **Mindful Listening:** The next time you're in a conversation, really listen. Don't just wait for your turn to speak—focus on the words, the tone, and the emotions behind what the other person is saying. This practice not only deepens your connection with others but also cultivates a habit of presence in your interactions. (Think of it as a mental upgrade from buffering to full streaming mode.)

→ **Mindful Observation:** Take a few minutes each day to simply observe your surroundings. Notice the colors, shapes, and patterns around you. Observe how the light changes throughout the day or how nature subtly shifts with the seasons. This practice trains your mind to stay present and appreciate the beauty of the moment. (Yes, that means actually looking up from your phone—crazy, right?)

Mindfulness bridges the gap between the physical and the spiritual. By integrating mindfulness into your life, you're not just calming your mind—you're tuning in to the frequency of your soul, setting the stage for all the spiritual insights and experiences to come. It's the foundation upon which a life of ease, authenticity, and spiritual connection is built. So, take a deep breath, settle into the moment, and see where this journey takes you.

FAITH IN A POWER SOURCE

Let's talk about faith—not necessarily in a religious sense, but in trusting that there's something greater than ourselves at play. Whether you call it the universe, God, source energy, or the mystery of life, having faith can be a game changer. It's like trusting that your well-chosen ingredients will create something delicious, even if you're not watching the pot. You've done your part, and now it's time to let the universe work its magic. Who knows? You might end up with something far better than you ever imagined.

Picture an invisible force gently guiding your life's path. It's beyond your control, and that's the beauty of it. In a world where we're told to manage every detail, faith invites you to lean back, stop micromanaging, and trust that things are unfolding as they should. How much stress comes from thinking we're solely responsible for everything? Faith is like a deep exhalation, reminding us that we can't control it all, and that's perfectly okay.

This isn't about giving up your agency. Faith encourages inspired action, knowing that whatever happens, it's part of a bigger design. It's a comforting safety net, allowing you to take risks without fearing unforgivable failure. Faith whispers that even if things don't go as planned, there's a reason, a lesson, or an unexpected opportunity waiting for you. Isn't it a relief to know you don't have to carry the weight of the world alone? There's a force—call it what you will—that's guiding you toward your highest good, even when the path seems unclear or messy. Faith isn't about giving up; it's about finding peace in the balance between what you can and can't control. It's about embracing the unknown with trust and curiosity, not fear.

SOUL-CENTERED LIVING

Let's revisit the difference between soul-centered and self-centered living. We touched on this concept in chapter 3 when we discussed the importance of making soul-centered investments in yourself. Now, let's explore it through a spiritual lens.

Go back to the proverbial meal we are cooking in this book. A self-centered approach is like following a recipe to the letter, even if it doesn't suit your taste or dietary needs. You might end up with a dish that looks great on Instagram, but it leaves you unsatisfied and longing for something more. On the other hand, a soul-centered approach is like cooking with intuition—choosing ingredients that nourish you, adjusting the recipe based on what feels right, and savoring the process as much as the final dish. This meal might not be what everyone else is making, but it's exactly what you need, and it leaves you feeling fulfilled and content. This distinction is important, especially in the context of spirituality and ease. **Life Lesson:** Self-centered desires and practices are usually driven by the ego—the part of us that craves validation, control, and quick-fix solutions. Soul-centered living is about playing the long game.

Let's break this concept down with a little help from Pixar's *Soul*. (Because who doesn't love a good animated existential crisis? And no, it will not be the last of my Pixar references—sorry, not sorry!) The main character, Joe, spends most of the movie chasing a dream he believes will finally make his life complete: playing jazz in a famous band. He's convinced that once he achieves this goal, everything will fall into place, and he'll feel whole. (Spoilers ahead!) When he finally gets there, it doesn't feel as fulfilling as he thought it would. It's like going to a restaurant you've been waiting to get into for ages, only to find the food tastes a bit bland, the waitstaff is rude, and the bill sets you back for a week.

Joe's journey is a perfect example of self-centered desires at play. He's so focused on this one goal, believing it's the key to his happiness, that he overlooks the richness of life happening all around him. It's like chasing after a mirage—it looks promising from a distance but disappears when you get close, leaving you thirsting for something more substantial. But the real magic happens after an unexpected accident encourages Joe to start shifting his perspective. Instead of being consumed by the idea of success, he begins to appreciate the small, everyday moments—the things that truly bring him joy and connect him to his inner self. It's in these moments of soul-centered living, when he's aligned with his true passions and seeing the world from a cat's perspective, that he finds real fulfillment.

And then there's 22, the character who initially has no interest in living a human life. She doesn't see the point until she starts to experience the simple pleasures of being alive—like feeling the wind on her face or tasting pizza for the first time. Her journey is all about discovering what it means to connect with the essence of life, and it's a beautiful reminder that fulfillment comes not from grand achievements but from embracing the present moment and finding joy in the little things.

Both Joe's and 22's stories remind us that when we live from a soul-centered place, rather than chasing after external fulfillment, we tap into a deeper, more meaningful experience of life. When you find your spark, you can let it guide your journey—not just to your goals but to a life that feels authentically yours. When your soul's experience guides you, every step you take feels aligned with something greater and more profound. It goes beyond achieving to becoming, evolving, and living in a way that feels more in harmony with who you want to be.

So, how do you know if you're living a soul-centered life? It starts with tuning in to what truly matters to you—not what society says you should want but what makes your heart sing. Reflect on times when you pursued something because it felt right, even if it didn't make logical sense. Those were the moments when you were aligned with your soul. The more you align with your soul, the more ease you'll experience, because you won't be fighting against the current of your true nature.

To activate living from a soul-centered place, begin by asking yourself:

1. **What are my core values?** These are your nonnegotiables, the flavors of your soul.

2. **What activities make me lose track of time?** These are often the things that connect you to your soul, get you into the flow state, and activate pleasure or your zone of genius— what you're good at and what you love.

3. **What dreams or desires have I put on the back burner because they didn't seem practical?** These soul-centered intentions are worth revisiting, as they may hold insight into your higher purpose if you are feeling unfulfilled, burned out, or lost.

INTUITION VS. INTRUSIVE THOUGHTS: NAVIGATING THE SPIRITUAL BATTLEFIELD

Let's dive into one of the trickiest parts of spirituality: understanding the difference between intuition and intrusive thoughts. This isn't just a psychology lesson; it's a spiritual necessity. Why? Because intuition is that inexplicable voice that guides us toward our higher purpose. It's the whisper that says, "This is the way," even when logic can't quite catch up. And if you can't hear or trust that voice, the spiritual practices we discuss later might feel like empty rituals. They're designed to strengthen your connection to intuition, but first, you need to recognize and understand that inner guidance.

Intuition is like your spiritual GPS—constantly recalculating to guide you down your true path. It works hand in hand with your clarity compass, which helps you navigate by aligning your actions with your values and goals. While your clarity compass sets the direction, intuition provides those subtle course corrections, steering you toward the decisions and opportunities that resonate with your deeper self. Intuition connects you to your purpose.

But unlike the clear, robotic directions from your car's GPS, intuition is subtle, almost elusive. It doesn't come with step-by-step instructions. Instead, it's a quiet knowing, a gut feeling that something is either right or wrong, often without a shred of tangible evidence to back it up. And that's what makes it so powerful—and so frustrating for those of us who like a little more proof before we jump into something.

On the flip side, intrusive thoughts are like the pop-up ads in your mind—annoying, distracting, and completely irrelevant to what you're trying to do. They're the thoughts that tell you you're not good enough, that you're going to fail, or that you shouldn't trust yourself. If left unchecked, they can easily pull you off course, making your spiritual journey feel like a never-ending obstacle course.

Intrusive thoughts often masquerade as guidance. Like static on the radio, they interrupt the clear signal of your intuition, making you second-guess yourself. These thoughts are usually born out of fear, anxiety, or past traumas, and they often sound like a broken record of self-doubt: *What if this goes wrong? You're not good enough for this. What if they don't like you?*

Imagine you're contemplating a career change that excites you, but doubts like *What if you fail?* or *You won't make enough money* flood your mind. These are intrusive thoughts, feeding on your fears and insecurities. They thrive on uncertainty, making you second-guess every step. In contrast, intuition speaks from a place of calm and clarity, often as a quiet but firm sense of knowing, like *This feels right* or *I need to pursue this.* It's that gentle nudge encouraging you to take the leap, even without all the answers.

Life Lesson: No one can really explain intuition. There's no scientific evidence for why we just know things sometimes. It's this mystical part of the human experience that defies logic, yet it's been the driving force behind countless "miracles" and life-changing decisions. When you listen to your intuition, it's like the universe starts conspiring in your favor. But if you can't hear it—or, worse, if you don't trust it—you end up taking the hard road, facing unnecessary struggles and obstacles that you could have avoided.

So, how do you get in touch with this mystical inner voice? Here are a few suggestions to get you started.

→ **Meditate Moderately: Your Spiritual Station**
   Meditation isn't just about zoning out or trying to "empty your mind." (Seriously, who can do that every day?) Meditation is about slowing down

and closing the mental tabs cluttering your mind, allowing for a fresh start. Picture your intuition as a cosmic radio station: you need to turn down the noise of daily life to catch the signal. Anything that allows you to calm your mind—even something as simple as gentle walking or cooking—can help you get into a meditative state. Start with just five minutes a day. Sit comfortably, close your eyes, and focus on your breath. Or if you choose to be in motion (please don't close your eyes), return to the breath as an anchor. Noticing your breathing alone can be a meditative practice. If your mind starts to wander (which it will), gently guide it back to your breath. It's like finding the perfect station with all your favorite hits—except these tunes are guiding your life.

→ **Pay Attention to Your Body: Your Spiritual GPS**
Your body is more than just a vehicle for your soul—it's like your spiritual GPS, giving you real-time updates on whether you're heading in the right direction. Ever get that gut feeling or a tingle down your spine? That's not just biology; it's your spirit trying to send you a message. For instance, if a decision makes you feel light and bubbly, it's probably your soul giving you the green light. But if you feel like you've swallowed a lead balloon, maybe it's time to reconsider. Your body's reactions are like those blinking arrows on a GPS screen, guiding you toward the path that's most aligned with your higher purpose. And the better you care for your body, as we discussed in chapter 5, the clearer the path to receiving useful directions. (And no, this doesn't mean you have to start doing yoga on a mountaintop—just start paying attention to how your body feels and let it be your guide.)

→ **Practice Discernment: Your Spiritual Gatekeeper**
Discernment is like your spiritual bouncer—
deciding which thoughts get VIP access to your
mind. Start practicing by taking a mental inventory
throughout the day. When a thought pops up,
especially if it's one that makes you feel uneasy or
anxious, ask yourself: Is this thought empowering
or disempowering? If it's the latter, imagine your
spiritual bouncer escorting it out of the club. For
example, if you're facing a decision and your mind
starts spiraling into worst-case scenarios, take a
step back and evaluate: Is this fear talking, or is it
your intuition giving you a gentle nudge? Over time,
you'll become better at recognizing which thoughts
deserve your attention and which ones are just
noise. (And you might realize your crazier party
days have been swapped for a cozy night in.)

→ **Journal Your Thoughts: Your Spiritual Diary**
Journaling isn't just for recording your daily
drama—it's your spiritual diary, where you can
connect with your inner self. Grab that beautiful
notebook you've been saving (yes, the one you've
been too afraid to write in) and start by jotting down
your thoughts and feelings. Set aside a few minutes
each day to write freely—don't censor yourself.
As you review your entries, look for patterns or
recurring themes. For instance, you might notice
that you feel most connected to your intuition
after spending time in nature or during quiet
moments in the morning. Use these insights to
strengthen your connection with your spiritual side.

→ **Trust the Process: Your Spiritual Muscle**
Intuition is like a spiritual muscle—the more you
use it, the stronger it gets. Start by acting on small,

intuitive nudges. Maybe it's reaching out to a friend you've been thinking about or taking a different route home just because it feels right. Each time you trust your gut, you're telling the universe you're ready to listen. Even if you're unsure of the outcome, take a leap of faith and trust that your intuition is guiding you toward your highest good. Over time, these small acts of trust will build your confidence in following your inner voice.

Connecting with your intuition means embracing life's mysteries and letting your inner wisdom guide you. It's about aligning with your soul's frequency to make your spiritual practices meaningful rather than hollow rituals. When I speak of something as "spiritual," I'm referring to the deeper connection between your inner self and a higher purpose. I'm emphasizing that your physical and intuitive sensations aren't just random—they're tied to a deeper wisdom that can guide you if you're willing to listen.

CONNECTING WITH YOUR HIGHER PURPOSE: MORE THAN A SPARK

Let's shift gears and talk about higher purpose—a concept that can feel a bit elusive, especially if you're not sure what yours is or whether you even believe in the idea. But here's a truth I've come to accept and back up: everyone has a higher purpose, even if it's not immediately obvious. Your higher purpose is the unique way you contribute to the world, and it's deeply connected to your soul-centered intentions.

For those who struggle with the idea of a higher purpose, think of it as the thing that makes you come alive, that drives you to get out of bed in the morning with a sense of excitement and meaning. It's not necessarily about grand gestures or world-changing achievements; sometimes, your higher purpose is simply about being kind, spreading joy, or creating beauty in your own unique way. Many of us equate higher purpose with our goals and "what we do." But when someone asks me what I do, I often ask for clarity: "What do I do for work? Or what do I do to live?"

There's a notable difference between these questions! Maybe your professional work is a conduit or a vehicle of your higher purpose. Maybe your work embodies your higher purpose completely. Or maybe what you do for work has absolutely nothing to do with how you experience your aliveness and what you contribute to the world by being yourself.

Let's circle back to the movie *Soul* for a second. Remember the character 22? She starts to spiral into becoming a lost soul because she convinces herself that she doesn't have a purpose, thinking she wasn't good enough. It's like she was searching for some specific talent she should have but just couldn't find. The movie shows us that a soul's "spark" isn't about nailing down a particular skill or being the best at something; it's more about what lights you up, what fuels your existence. And here's the thing: you have to keep that spark alive. The lost souls in the movie are a powerful reminder of what happens when we let go of our desires and passions. We end up in a loop of doubt and regret, stuck in a place where we're just existing, not really living. The truth is, a soul's purpose is to find the unique path that feels right to you.

But how do you discover this higher purpose if it feels out of reach? Start by exploring what you're naturally drawn to. What activities or causes ignite a fire in you? What do you love doing so much that you'd do it for free? These are clues regarding your higher purpose. If you're feeling lost, remember that your higher purpose isn't something you have to find all at once. It's a journey of discovery, and it often unfolds gradually over time as you follow your intuition and soul-centered desires. **Life Lesson:** No matter what others tell you about what you *should* do, only you can truly know and feel your higher purpose.

Connecting with your higher purpose isn't really something I can give you an exact recipe for, but here are some cooking tips that can help you create your own recipe:

→ **Reflect on your passions.** What are you passionate about? What makes your heart race and your soul light up? (And no, I'm not talking about that third cup of coffee.) These passions are often breadcrumbs leading you toward your higher purpose. When you dig into what you genuinely care about, you'll find the core of what drives you.

→ **Where do you feel most "you"?** Think about the environments, people, or activities that make you feel most like yourself. When do you feel you can truly breathe and be authentic? (If you're picturing yourself in pajamas binge-watching Netflix, hey, no judgment, but maybe dig a little deeper.) Noting where your authentic self feels safe and active is a big clue regarding where your higher purpose might be hiding.

→ **Seek out experiences.** Put yourself out there—go for that new job, take that art class, or try surfing for the first time. It's in these new and sometimes uncomfortable situations that you discover more about what truly matters to you. Plus, you'll probably collect some great stories along the way (or at least a few good laughs at your expense). Put yourself in new situations that challenge what you think or know about yourself.

→ **Trust the process.** Your higher purpose isn't going to just knock on your door one day and introduce itself (though wouldn't that be nice?). It will reveal itself over time, through experiences, challenges, and those little intuitive nudges that guide you toward what feels right. Be patient and keep following those breadcrumbs—even if it sometimes feels like you're just wandering through the forest or staring blankly into the fridge, hoping dinner will make itself.

→ **Ask for feedback.** This one might feel a bit intense (or morbid, depending on how you spin it), but it's incredibly insightful: ask your trusted loved ones what they think you bring to their lives. How do you impact others? What will they remember you for? Sometimes, it's easier to see your higher purpose reflected in the eyes of those who know you best. (And hey, you might even get a little ego boost out of it—win-win!)

FINDING MAGIC IN THE MUNDANE

Synchronicity is the universe's way of saying, "Hey, I see you!"—moments when life feels like it's playing along with your story. Picture this: you think of an old friend, and suddenly they text you, or you keep seeing the same numbers everywhere, like 11:11. Even if you convince yourself that it's just the time on the clock, for that split second, you're pulled out of the ordinary, and suddenly, you're connected to something larger than yourself. This concept is my absolute favorite because it makes life feel like an interactive adventure. It's like having a cosmic ally walking with you on the existential yellow brick road.

These synchronicities can be anything—a random song on the radio that speaks to exactly what you're feeling, a book falling off the shelf that answers a question you've been pondering, or a stranger's passing comment that seems to be just for you. It's like getting a secret message from the universe, one that only you can decode. It turns the mundane into the magical and makes every day feel like an opportunity for connection and meaning. When you start noticing these signs, it's as if the universe is saying, "Keep going; you're not alone in this." They serve as gentle reminders that there's a deeper rhythm to life, one that your intuition is tuned in to.

Let me share a little story about the number twenty-two and how it became a guiding light during one of the most transformative times in my life. It all started in a whirlwind when I was scrambling to renew my passport on the same day I was supposed to catch a redeye flight to Mexico for a soul activation retreat. Naturally, I only realized my passport had expired a few days before—classic, right? So there I was, racing between the passport office and home, anxiously hoping to get everything sorted in time. That's when the number twenty-two started showing up. At first, I noticed it on the clock—always (hour):22. Then on buses, on license plates, and even on my ticket number at the passport office.

It wasn't just a coincidence; it felt like the universe was waving a flag at me. I got my passport just in time, made the flight, and I settled into my seat—yep, you guessed it—seat 22. That trip and retreat became a pivotal moment, opening my eyes to the life I truly wanted. And when I returned home, the number kept appearing in random places at meaningful moments (so often and in such uncanny ways that even the skeptics around me started to believe and notice the sign surrounding me).

The movie *Soul* came out soon after this chapter of my life, and the character named 22 resonated deeply with me. Her journey of discovering the beauty in simply living paralleled my own experience of learning to find joy in the ordinary. As synchronicities like seeing the number twenty-two everywhere continued, they became guiding signs, reminding me I was on the right path. These moments, though small, added a layer of magic and meaning to my life, connecting me to something greater and reinforcing the belief that I was exactly where I needed to be.

Now, I see synchronicities all the time. They're my new normal because I've learned to be open to them. I enjoy them, and they make my life feel like it's filled with a little bit of magic, something far from average. Signs and synchronicities are powerful when you let them be. They're like little puzzles from the universe. Whether you choose to believe in them or not, they have the power to make your life feel connected to something beyond yourself, something more meaningful. And if you're open to them, they just might become a ritual in your life, leading you to exactly where you're meant to be.

RITUALS: RIDING THE RHYTHM

Rituals go beyond habits—they're sacred practices that infuse life with intention and connection to something greater. Unlike habits, which are about routine, rituals elevate our daily actions by making them meaningful. For instance, making your bed can be a habit, but turning it into a ritual means setting an intention for your day as you do it. Rituals provide structure and rhythm, helping us slow down, be present, and connect with the divine. They honor both the ordinary and extraordinary, reminding us that even small actions can hold profound significance. While daily habits are the building blocks of our routines, rituals are the practices that elevate those routines to something more profound. Rituals enhance and add ease to life by providing structure and rhythm. By integrating rituals into our lives, we're not just repeating actions for tradition's sake; we're participating in living history, connecting with our roots, and creating a sense of spiritual grounding that can make life feel more meaningful—and yes, easier.

Rituals have been essential to human life since civilization's dawn, marking significant events, honoring the divine, and fostering communal bonds. From ancient ceremonies to modern practices like lighting candles for various cultural celebrations, rituals connect us to our ancestors and provide continuity in an ever-changing world. These timeless practices fulfill our need for meaning, guiding us through life's challenges with grace and celebrating its joys with intention. By integrating rituals into our lives, we honor the journey we're on and the sacredness of each moment.

THE GENTRIFICATION AND CULTURAL APPROPRIATION OF RITUALS

However, as rituals from different cultures have gained popularity in mainstream society, there has been a growing issue of gentrification and cultural appropriation. Practices that hold deep spiritual significance for one group are often adopted by another, sometimes in ways that strip them of their original meaning or context. This can be seen in the widespread use of smudging with sage, a sacred practice among many Indigenous peoples in North America. While smudging has become trendy in wellness communities, it's important to remember that this ritual is rooted in specific cultural and spiritual traditions that deserve respect and understanding.

To engage in rituals with respect and awareness, try the following:

1. **Do your research.** Before adopting a ritual from another culture, take the time to learn about its origins, its significance, and how it is traditionally practiced. For example, if you're interested in using *palo santo*, research its traditional use in South American Indigenous cultures and the environmental impact of its rising demand. (*Pro tip:* Searching Wikipedia is a place to start, but also dive deeper into books, articles, and, if possible, conversations with people from the culture you're learning about. The goal is to understand, not just to consume.)

2. **Ask for permission.** If you're engaging with rituals from a culture that's not your own, it's respectful to ask for permission or seek guidance from someone who is part of that culture. For instance, if you're attending a sweat lodge ceremony, understand that you're in a sacred space, and it's essential to follow the guidance of the leader, who is often a spiritual elder. (And no, asking your friend who took one hot yoga class doesn't count. Find someone who truly understands the cultural significance.)

3. **Support authentic sources.** When purchasing items like sage, crystals, or ceremonial tools, buy from Indigenous or local artisans who use sustainable practices. This not only ensures that you're getting authentic products but also supports the communities from which these rituals come. (Because if you're buying sage from a big-box retailer, you might as well be buying your "authentic" sushi from a gas station—just don't.)

4. Acknowledge the source. When you incorporate a ritual into your practice, acknowledge where it comes from and express gratitude for the culture that has shared it. This could be as simple as a moment of silence before you begin or a prayer of thanks. (Think of it like crediting the recipe creator when you share your kitchen masterpiece.)

EXAMPLES OF RESPECTFUL RITUAL IMMERSION

→ **Prayer:** Prayer is one of the oldest rituals, practiced across nearly every culture in the world. It's not just about asking for things; it's a moment to connect with the divine, express gratitude, seek guidance, or simply acknowledge that you're part of something greater than yourself. Prayer doesn't need to be confined to traditional religious settings—it can be done quietly in your mind or spoken aloud, directed to whomever or whatever you believe in, and it can be about anything that's on your heart. (**Life Lesson:** Don't stress about finding the "right" words—prayer is more about sincerity than eloquence. And remember, it's okay to mix things up; your prayer practice can be as formal or as casual as you need it to be.)

→ **Mantras:** Repeating a mantra is like setting your brain on a calming loop. Whether you're chanting a traditional Sanskrit mantra like "Om Shanti" or simply repeating a personal affirmation like "I am enough," the magic lies in the repetition and the intention behind it. It's like tuning your inner radio to the frequency of peace and clarity, helping to drown out the static of everyday worries. (*Pro tip:* Try using a *mala*—a string of 108

beads—to count your repetitions. It's meditation
with a side of style and helps you stay focused
and accountable by using a physical tool.)

→ **Meditation:** Meditation is the ultimate ritual
for cultivating inner peace, strengthening your
intuition, and fortifying clarity. Whether you're
practicing mindfulness, focusing on your breath,
or visualizing your goals, meditation helps quiet
the mind and center the spirit. It's like giving your
brain a much-needed vacation from the chaos
of daily life. (*Pro tip:* If you're new to meditation,
start small—just five minutes a day can make
a big difference. And don't get discouraged if
your mind wanders. That's totally normal. The
key is to gently bring your focus back again
and again. Plus, there's no such thing as a bad
meditation session; it's all part of the process.)

→ **Ceremonies:** Ceremonies are the spiritual
equivalent of life's bookmarks. They mark the
passages of time, honor transitions, and help us
align with the cycles of nature. Whether it's a
full moon ceremony (more on that in a minute), a
seasonal solstice celebration, or a personal rite of
passage like a birthday, wedding, or graduation,
ceremonies give us a chance to pause, reflect,
and connect with something deeper. (*Pro tip:*
Create your own personal ceremonies—light
a candle on significant dates, journal your
intentions, create a vision board at the start of
each month, or simply celebrate the start of a
new season with a nature walk. Bonus points for
sharing your new traditions with loved ones.)

→ **Retreats:** One of my all-time favorite rituals is
retreating—literally retreating away from the

world to return to myself. There's nothing quite like hitting the spiritual reset button, and retreats are the perfect way to do just that. You've got the classic options like weekend meditation retreats, yoga getaways, or solo trips into nature. But don't be too quick to dismiss the less conventional retreats out there—think soul activation retreats, adult summer camps, silence retreats, or even more niche experiences like sapphic gatherings, holistic wellness retreats, music or writing retreats, and couples retreats for those brave enough to dive deeper into their relationships. On retreats, I have discovered some of the most profound self-insights, been inspired by some of my most sacred ideas, and connected with some of the best people I know. Retreats offer a unique opportunity to disconnect from the daily grind and reconnect with your inner self. It's like giving your soul a day at the spa—only instead of a facial, you're getting a full spiritual makeover. (*Pro tip:* When you're on retreat, leave your to-do list at the door. This is your time to be present, so resist the urge to check emails or update your Instagram every five minutes. Trust me, the world will keep spinning even if you're off-grid for a bit.)

→ **EFT Tapping:** Emotional Freedom Technique (EFT) tapping can help you balance and restore your energy throughout the day, keeping you centered and calm. The technique, which has roots in Traditional Chinese Medicine, involves tapping on specific acupressure points on the body while focusing on an issue you'd like to resolve—whether it's stress, anxiety, or physical pain. This practice can be like a quick reset button for your mind and body. Start by identifying an issue you want to work on. Tap gently with your fingertips on the following points: the side of your hand (often called the "karate chop" point), the top of your head, your eyebrows, the sides of your eyes, under your eyes, under your nose, your chin, your collarbone, and under your arm. As you tap each point, repeat a statement that acknowledges the issue and affirms your acceptance of yourself, such as "I am capable" or "I am safe." (*Pro tip:* You can practice EFT anytime and anywhere. It might feel a little awkward at first to tap in public, but this practice is helpful in overstimulating environments, so don't be afraid to tap when you need it.)

→ **Water Release Therapy®:** Rooted in the art of Watsu® and developed by Diane Feingold, Water Release Therapy® is a profound aquatic healing modality designed to release trauma and old patterns stored in the body and mind. This therapy combines the stillness of Watsu®, the fluidity of WaterDance, and elements of breathwork and yoga, creating a deeply transformative experience. In warm water, you're guided through a journey of somatic release, often involving moments when you're gently taken underwater, allowing for the dissolution of physical and emotional boundaries. Diane's healing touch and presence make this therapy a unique opportunity for deep healing and integration. As I am now certified in WRT Water Release Therapy® under Diane's mentorship, I can't recommend the method enough for those seeking profound healing and a renewed sense of self. The water greets and holds you, unlike any other method I've experienced before. (*Pro tip:* When you step into the warm water, let your body melt like butter on hot toast—just surrender completely and let your heart do the navigating. Trust the water and your facilitator to take you on a journey during which your mind can take a backseat and your body can unwind. The deeper you let go, the more magic happens. And fair warning: this kind of deep relaxation works up a serious hunger, so have a snack ready for afterward—you'll need it!)

→ **Celtic Weave Technique:** The Celtic Weave is an ancient practice rooted in Celtic traditions that is believed to help balance the body's energy fields. It's a simple yet powerful technique that can be incorporated into daily rituals to promote well-being and ease. The Celtic Weave involves moving your hands in a figure-eight pattern around your body. This pattern is thought to weave together the energies within and around you, aligning your physical and energetic bodies. To perform the Celtic Weave, stand with your feet shoulder-width apart, arms at your sides. Inhale deeply, and as you exhale, bring your hands up in front of your body, crossing them at the wrists. With your hands still crossed, move them in a figure-eight pattern, allowing the motion to flow naturally. Continue this figure-eight motion, moving your arms up and down your body, imagining that you are weaving together the energies that surround you. After a few moments, bring your hands back to your sides, take a deep breath, and feel the balanced energy within and around you. This simple practice can be done daily or whenever you feel the need to balance your energy. (*Pro tip:* The Celtic Weave is great when you first get out of bed and want to wake up your body and spirit. It serves as a reminder of the interconnectedness of all things and can help you feel more grounded and centered.)

→ **Yoga:** Yoga is a spiritual practice with roots in ancient India. While it's become a global phenomenon, it's essential to remember that yoga is not just about physical postures but also about breathwork, meditation, and ethical living. When practicing yoga, try to honor its roots by learning about its philosophical background and incorporating mindfulness into your practice. (*Pro tip:* Dive into the eight limbs of yoga—it's not just about nailing that headstand. The physical postures, or asanas, are just one part of a much broader spiritual practice. Explore the other limbs—like pranayama or breath control, dhyana or meditation, and yamas or ethical guidelines—to truly experience the depth and wisdom that yoga offers. Embracing these elements can transform your practice from just a workout into a holistic journey toward inner peace and self-awareness.)

→ **Smudging:** If you choose to smudge with sage or other sacred herbs, do so with the reverence and respect the practice deserves. Understand its significance, and avoid using it as just a "trendy" way to clear bad vibes. Always leave the area you're cleansing with gratitude for the protection and guidance offered. (*Pro tip:* White sage is endangered, so maybe opt for ethically sourced or alternative herbs like cedar or sweetgrass.)

→ **Sound Baths/Healing:** Sound baths are a deeply immersive and meditative experience, often involving the soothing vibrations of crystal bowls, gongs, and other instruments that wash over you, helping to balance your energy and bring about deep relaxation. Participating in a sound bath is like letting your entire being soak in the healing frequencies of sound, allowing the vibrations to clear away stress and restore harmony to your body and mind. (*Pro tip:* When attending a sound bath, set an intention before you begin. Whether it's to release tension, gain clarity, or simply relax, having a clear focus can enhance the experience and deepen your connection to the healing process.)

→ **Reiki:** Reiki is a form of energy healing that originated in Japan, where a practitioner channels healing energy into the client's body through their hands, often without physical touch. It's like a gentle, energetic massage that helps to release blockages and restore balance. Reiki can be a profound way to connect with your body's natural ability to heal itself, promoting overall well-being and spiritual alignment. (*Pro tip:* After a Reiki session, take some time to rest and hydrate. The energy work can bring up emotions or physical sensations, so it's important to listen to your body and give yourself the space to integrate the healing.)

→ **Ayahuasca or Plant Medicine Ceremonies:** These ceremonies are deeply rooted in traditional Amazonian spiritual practices. As they gain popularity in the West, it's essential to approach them with respect, ideally under the guidance of a trained shaman who understands the cultural and spiritual significance of the medicine. If you choose to participate, do so with a deep respect for the shaman's approach, acknowledging the extensive training and experience they've undergone to offer this sacred practice. Undergoing deep psychoactive and hallucinogenic experiences can offer insight into more profound subconscious questions and grant a deeper access to the parts of your psyche. (*Pro tip:* Before participating in an ayahuasca ceremony, have a conversation with the shaman or facilitator about your intentions and your desire

to work with the plant medicine. This dialogue
not only shows respect for the tradition but also
deepens your experience, enabling you to receive
more profound insights and healing during the
ceremony. And follow the diet ahead of time—your
body and your purge bucket will thank you later!)

→ **Altar Creation:** Creating a personal altar is a
beautiful and intentional way to honor your spiritual
practice. Think of it as your sacred corner, a
dedicated space where you can place meaningful
objects that inspire you and help you connect with
your spiritual side. This could include crystals
that resonate with your energy, candles that
symbolize light and clarity, photos of loved ones
or mentors who uplift you, or sacred texts that
offer wisdom and guidance. Essentially, your altar
becomes a physical representation of your spiritual
journey—a place where your outer world meets
your inner world. (*Pro tip:* Keep your altar dynamic
by changing it with the seasons or whenever
you feel like you need a fresh burst of energy.
You could add flowers in spring, sun symbols
in summer, autumn leaves in fall, and perhaps
evergreen branches or snowflakes in winter. And
remember, there's no right or wrong way to create
an altar—it's all about what resonates with you.
Your altar is a reflection of your unique spiritual
path, so make it a space that truly feels like yours.)

→ **Feng Shui:** The idea that a tidy living space leads
to a tidy mind isn't just a modern-day concept—
it's rooted in ancient wisdom, particularly in the
practice of feng shui, which originated in China
over three thousand years ago. Feng shui is all
about creating harmony between you and your
environment by optimizing the flow of energy, or

chi, in your space. A cluttered environment can create a mental fog, making it harder to focus and feel at ease, much like trying to cook in a messy kitchen—chaos everywhere. To apply feng shui principles in your home, start by decluttering and organizing your space. Keep pathways clear to allow energy to flow freely throughout your home. (*Pro tip:* When it comes to your bedroom, the bed should be positioned so that you can see the door without being directly in line with it—this is known as the "command position," and it promotes a sense of security and relaxation.)

→ **Journaling:** Keeping a spiritual journal is like having a conversation with your soul. It's a space to explore your thoughts, reflect on your experiences, and track your spiritual growth over time. You can use it to document your dreams, set intentions, or even just jot down the random insights that pop into your head. Journaling is a powerful tool for cultivating ease and authenticity and can complement the principles of any chapter in this book. By dedicating time to explore your mental, physical, and spiritual sides on paper, you give yourself the space to fully embrace and understand your life experiences. (*Pro tip:* Don't censor yourself. Let your thoughts flow freely onto the page—sometimes, the messiest entries hold the deepest wisdom. And who knows? Maybe your future self will look back on these pages and thank you for the breadcrumb trail of insights.)

CYCLES: EMBRACING THE FLOW

Let's talk about cycles. No, not the kind you ride in spin class—but the natural, spiritual, and life cycles that shape our existence. This section is less of a how-to and more of a good-to-know when cultivating ease. If there's one thing the moon and ancient wisdom teach us, it's that everything in life comes in phases, and understanding these cycles is helpful in living with authenticity and ease. There's a deep wisdom in looking to the natural world for guidance. The moon, for instance, waxes and wanes, symbolizing growth, fullness, release, and renewal. Just like the moon, our lives move through phases—times of growth and new beginnings and moments of rest, reflection, or release. Cycles are everywhere, reminding us that change is both inevitable and essential. Recognizing these rhythms helps us flow with life rather than resisting it. Life isn't a straight line; it's a series of waves. By honoring our personal rhythms, we understand when to push forward and when to pause, much like a chef who knows that some dishes need time to marinate for the best flavor.

THE CYCLICAL NATURE OF EASE

Here are a few ways that cycles illuminate the path toward ease.

→ **Connection to Nature:** Spirituality connects us to the natural world, aligning us with cycles like the moon's phases and the changing seasons, reminding us of our place in the universe.

→ **Personal Growth:** Just as nature goes through cycles, so do we. Recognizing these phases allows us to honor our personal growth at our own pace.

→ **Letting Go:** Like the waning moon, cycles teach us the importance of releasing what no longer serves us, creating space for new growth.

→ **Creating Rituals around Cycles:** Rituals aligned with natural cycles help us mark time, celebrate milestones, and stay connected to the universe's rhythm. (**Life Lesson:** Use these ceremonies as your personal "reset" button—perfect for when life starts to feel like an overwhelming, never-ending to-do list.)

So, as you move through this chapter and beyond, remember that it's okay to have days when you're not at your peak. Just like the moon isn't always full, you don't have to be either. Embrace your cycles, celebrate your phases, and know that each one is vital in letting life be easy. I'm going to touch on the moon (this is the spiritual chapter—we have to talk about the moon!), but let's chat a little bit more about the cycle that likes to make a monthly visit.

MENSTRUATION: THE SACRED CYCLE

Menstruation and the cycles of pregnancy are profound experiences that connect women deeply to the rhythms of nature. These cycles aren't just biological; they are spiritual opportunities for renewal and self-reflection. In many cultures, menstruation has been revered as a sacred process, symbolizing the divine feminine and the life-death-rebirth cycle. Ancient rituals like moon lodges allowed women to honor this time through rest and introspection. (My backyard shed might need some moon lodge renovations!) Today, some women are reclaiming these practices, transforming menstruation into a personal ceremony for self-care and spiritual connection. This shift reframes menstruation from a burden to a celebration of life's natural rhythms. The menstrual cycle can be broken down into four distinct phases, each offering unique insights and opportunities for personal growth.

Understanding these phases might help you make this cycle a superpower as you embrace the life of ease you're creating.

1. **Menstrual Phase (Winter)**
   This is the phase most people are familiar with—the actual period. It's a time of shedding, not just physically but emotionally and spiritually as well. This phase mirrors the energy of winter—a time for introspection, rest, and release. It's an opportunity to let go of what no longer serves you and to reset your intentions for the next cycle. During this time, it's essential to give yourself permission to slow down, to rest more, and to honor the body's need for renewal. (*Pro tip:* Don't push yourself to be productive during this phase. Embrace the downtime, and let your body lead the way.)

2. **Follicular Phase (Spring)**
   Following menstruation, the follicular phase is like the arrival of spring. Energy levels begin to rise, and there's a sense of renewal and possibility. This is a great time to start new projects, set goals, and engage in activities that require creativity and enthusiasm. Your body is preparing for ovulation, and the hormonal changes support a sense of optimism and focus. (*Pro tip:* Use this phase to brainstorm, plan, and take the first steps toward your goals. It's your body's natural time for growth and new beginnings.)

3. **Ovulation Phase (Summer)**
   Ovulation is the peak of the cycle—the body's equivalent of summertime. It's a time of heightened energy, socialization, and outward expression. During this phase, you might feel more confident, attractive, and ready to

connect with others. It's also a time when your body is most fertile, symbolizing creativity and abundance. (*Pro tip:* This is a great time for collaboration, networking, and putting yourself out there. Use the heightened energy to pursue your passions and connect with others.)

4. **Luteal Phase (Fall)**
   As the body prepares to either begin menstruation or support early pregnancy, the luteal phase mirrors the energy of fall. It's a time for winding down, finishing projects, and taking stock of what you've accomplished. This phase often brings a heightened awareness of emotions and a need for self-care. It's a good time to focus on tasks that require attention to detail and to start turning inward again. (*Pro tip:* Practice self-care and mindfulness during this phase. It's your body's way of telling you to slow down and prepare for the next cycle.)

There's a growing body of literature that explores how to live in harmony with your menstrual cycle, offering insights into how this natural rhythm affects everything from work and nutrition to sex and general daily activities. Books like *The Fifth Vital Sign* by Lisa Hendrickson-Jack and *In the FLO* by Alisa Vitti provide guidance on how to harness the power of your menstrual cycle to optimize your life. By recognizing the wisdom in these phases, you can live more in tune with your body's natural rhythms, creating a life that feels more aligned, authentic, and easy. Whether it's adjusting your schedule, nourishing your body with the right foods, or simply giving yourself permission to rest, honoring your menstrual cycle is a powerful way to embrace your true self and make life a little easier.

THE MOON: THE SOUL CYCLE

Alright, I wanted to discuss menstruation and pregnancy with as much reverence, respect, and honor as I could. But in talking about the moon, I've got to be a bit more candid. Yes, many of these cycles are influenced by the moon, and there's a reason why the woo-woo crowd gets called out for their moon obsessions. Even in psychology, we've debated whether the moon plays a role in the behavior of "lunatics" (a term rooted in the idea that the moon causes madness) and whether the water in our bodies is affected by its cycles.

Now, I'm speaking to the skeptics here: I get it. Linking your well-being or natural life cycles with the moon can sound, well, a bit out there. But here's the thing: I operate under a philosophy of acceptance that if something exists, it does so for a reason. There must be enough people who've found significance and value in it for it to persist in our reality. (Now, don't jump down my throat—this philosophy can be applied to a lot of things, some of them not so great, but for the sake of ease, let's stick to the moon.)

I'm careful about how I express my relationship with the moon. Lean too far into it, and I'm pegged as a far-out, spacey type; lean too far the other way, and I deny the synchronicities that have shaped my own life. I've manifested desires on new moons that have come to pass, and I've watched my mind scramble under full moons. So, I felt it was important to include the moon in this chapter because, for many, it serves as a compass—a way to track their own cycles and better understand themselves.

I'm not saying you should strip down and dance under the next full moon (though I highly recommend it), nor am I suggesting that the celestial body dictates every miracle that happens in our little human lives. What I am saying is that there's a reason why so many people look to the moon in their quest for authenticity and ease. It's a tool, a guide, and a way to connect with something bigger. So, whether you're a die-hard believer or a skeptical observer, there's space here for you to explore what the moon—and these cycles—might mean for your own journey.

ASTROLOGY AND PERSONOLOGY: YOUR COSMIC BLUEPRINT

Personology delves into understanding the deeper aspects of our identity, blending mystical and psychological insights from systems such as astrology, Enneagram, and Human Design. These tools provide frameworks for self-awareness, helping us recognize patterns in our behavior and relationships. They connect us to the spiritual essence of who we are, offering clarity on our unique blueprint and guiding us toward living more authentically. But here's the thing: these methods of self-reflection aren't about fate; they're about potential. Their guidance is like getting a recipe from the universe, but you still get to decide how to cook it. Understanding your astrological chart or other profiles from personology can help you navigate life with more ease, providing you with more colors on your palette to craft an authentic life you're proud of. As a coach, I decided to set myself apart by incorporating astrology and personology into my approach. This isn't just about expanding horizons—it's about offering clients a broader perspective on their thoughts and needs. Plus, it gets to be fun!

For those who are open to it, astrology and personology can be powerful tools for understanding your personal journey and purpose. Think of them as your cosmic blueprint—guides to who you are and what you're here to do. Let's talk astrology—the ultimate cosmic recipe book. If you've ever wondered why some days you feel like a go-getter while others you're more inclined to hide under the covers, the stars might have something to do with it. Astrology is all about understanding the influence of celestial bodies on our lives, and while it's easy to dismiss as just a fun party trick, there's actually a rich tradition behind it that's worth exploring. Plus, it can be eerily accurate, and who doesn't love a little cosmic validation?

THE HiSTORiCAL CONTEXT OF ASTROLOGY

Astrology has been around for thousands of years, with its origins tracing back to ancient Babylon, where people first began to notice the correlation between celestial movements and earthly events. It spread to ancient Greece, where philosophers like Ptolemy wrote extensively on the subject, and eventually to India, where Vedic astrology developed its unique system. For much of history, astrology was considered a legitimate science, used by kings and scholars to make decisions about everything from agriculture to warfare. The practice of reading the stars was not just about predicting the future; it was about understanding the self. This belief persisted through the ages, even as astrology became less respected in the scientific community.

WHY PEOPLE USE ASTROLOGY

Astrology's resurgence in popular culture, especially over the past few decades, can be attributed to a few factors. As traditional religious practices decline, many people turn to astrology for spiritual insight and a sense of control in a complex world. The digital age has made astrology more accessible, with social media boosting its popularity. (Astrologers are thriving online, and card-pulling posts go viral!) Astrology offers a comforting narrative, helping people make sense of life's chaos and feel connected to something larger. It's no surprise that astrology's popularity surges during uncertain times.

When I was sixteen and grappling with the big questions of identity and purpose, astrology offered me a lifeline. No one around me seemed to have the answers I was looking for, and astrology gave me a language to describe traits and patterns I saw in myself. It provided a mirror, reflecting aspects of my personality that I couldn't quite articulate. Suddenly, there was evidence—however esoteric—that I wasn't alone in my experiences.

Astrology gets a bad name for being woo-woo or easily dismissed as pseudoscience. Many skeptics criticize it for oversimplifying the human experience, compartmentalizing the entire human race into twelve signs. But here's the thing: astrology, like many other forms of personology, is less about rigid definitions and more about exploring potentialities. It's a tool, not a doctrine. For those who embrace it, astrology offers insight into why you might be prone to certain behaviors, what challenges you might face, and how you can best navigate them. It's not about fatalism; it's about self-awareness.

Of course, astrology isn't for everyone, and it's important to approach it with a critical eye. It's easy to see why some might dismiss it as too vague or overly deterministic. But even if you don't buy into the idea that the stars control our destinies, there's value in the self-reflection that astrology encourages. It's not about predicting the future; it's about understanding the present—how you react to the world, how you relate to others, and what drives you. And if nothing else, it's always handy to have a celestial scapegoat when things don't go your way ("I'm sorry, I can't help it—Mercury's in retrograde," or my personal catchphrase: "Sorry, I'm a Leo.").

STAR SIGNS AND PERSONOLOGY

Astrology is more than just your sun sign—it's a comprehensive map that provides insights into your personality, strengths, challenges, and life path. Your astrological chart, which includes your sun, moon, and rising signs, along with the positions of other planets, is like a recipe unique to you, blending different ingredients that shape who you are. Understanding these elements can offer profound guidance on how to live more authentically and navigate life with greater ease. For example, knowing your sun sign reveals your core self, while your moon sign sheds light on your emotional world. Your rising sign influences how others perceive you, and each planet's position provides additional layers of insight. Recognizing these patterns can clarify why you connect with certain people and why specific challenges arise in your life. There is much to uncover once you dive deep into your natal chart, but below is a little taste of each sign.

→ **Aries (March 21–April 19):** The spicy chili pepper of the zodiac—bold, assertive, and a little bit hotheaded, Aries is a natural leader who dives headfirst into challenges. They're the one who orders the extra-hot salsa and doesn't break a sweat.

→ **Taurus (April 20–May 20):** The rich, decadent chocolate cake—sensual, grounded, and a lover of all things luxurious, Taurus knows how to enjoy the finer things in life. They savor every bite of that cake, refusing to rush the experience.

→ **Gemini (May 21–June 20):** The tapas plate—

variety is the spice of life for Gemini. Curious, adaptable, and great communicators, they're always sampling new ideas and experiences. Don't be surprised if they change their mind midmeal and ask for something completely different.

→ **Cancer (June 21–July 22):** The comforting bowl of soup—nurturing, empathetic, and a little bit moody, Cancer craves security and emotional warmth, much like that homemade meal that reminds you of home.

→ **Leo (July 23–August 22):** The show-stopping flambé—dramatic, confident, and the life of the party, Leo loves to shine, and they're not afraid to be the center of attention. Just don't forget to compliment the chef!

→ **Virgo (August 23–September 22):** The meticulously prepared salad—practical, detail-oriented, and health-conscious, Virgo loves order and precision, ensuring that every ingredient is perfectly balanced. They'll read the nutritional information before taking a bite.

→ **Libra (September 23–October 22):** The beautifully plated dessert—charming, balanced, and always aesthetically pleasing, Libra values harmony and beauty, making sure that every element of their life is as delightful as a perfectly arranged dessert.

→ **Scorpio (October 23–November 21):** The mysterious, spicy cocktail—intense, passionate, and a bit of an enigma, Scorpio dives deep into the hidden layers of life, savoring the complexity of flavors and emotions. They can't resist ordering the drink with the secret ingredient.

→ **Sagittarius (November 22–December 21):** The exotic, adventurous dish—free-spirited, optimistic, and always up for something new, Sagittarius loves to explore, whether it's new cuisines or new philosophies. They'll happily try the dish you can't even pronounce.

→ **Capricorn (December 22–January 19):** The classic, no-nonsense steak and potatoes—ambitious, disciplined, and traditional, Capricorn knows that success takes hard work, and they're willing to put in the effort to get the job done right.

→ **Aquarius (January 20–February 18):** The avant-garde fusion cuisine—innovative, unconventional, and always ahead of the curve, Aquarius is the visionary of the zodiac, blending flavors and ideas that others might not even think of. They inspire you to say, "I never thought of that, but it works!"

→ **Pisces (February 19–March 20):** The dreamy, ethereal soufflé—intuitive, compassionate, and a bit of a romantic, Pisces sees the world through rose-colored glasses, and their creativity adds a touch of magic to everything they do.

Beyond romantic compatibility, astrology can help you identify the best times to make major life decisions, like starting a new job, moving to a new city, or launching a creative project. It can also guide you in understanding your strengths and challenges, offering insights into your personal growth, career path, and even your approach to self-care. And let's not forget the fun stuff—like knowing when Mercury is in retrograde so you can brace yourself for those inevitable tech glitches and communication mishaps. (*Pro tip:* Don't sign contracts or buy electronics during this time unless you enjoy living on the edge.) So, while astrology may seem like a mystical art, it's also a practical tool that can help you navigate the ups and downs of life with a little more ease and a lot more humor. After all, if the stars are going to influence us, we might as well make the most of it, right?

MANIFESTATION: THE COSMIC RECIPE FOR MAKING LIFE DELICIOUSLY EASY

Crafting a life you're proud of involves various methods discussed throughout this book. One essential element is manifestation; think of it as the salt that enhances every recipe in each chapter. Manifestation is essentially the process you engage in when you express a desire for change, like wanting life to be easier. The "if you let it" part reflects the work and effort I offer in these pages, guiding you to embrace that ease. The "it gets to be easy" aspect is deeply intertwined with the principles of manifestation, layering your intentions with practical actions to bring them to life. Imagine you're in your kitchen, creating a recipe for your dream life (which you've been doing since chapter 1). Every intention you set is like choosing the perfect ingredient, and the energy you put into it is how you cook it all together. As you focus on what you truly want, the universe helps you mix it all up, bringing your vision to life. Every positive thought adds a sprinkle of magic seasoning, helping your goals come to fruition. By wanting ease, visualizing ease, and making changes that make life easier, you are manifesting, my dear.

In the context of spirituality, manifestation is like a warm hug from the universe. It reassures you that you're a cocreator of your life, not just a passive observer. When you manifest, you're tapping into the deeper truths of your own mind and soul. You're tuning in to what you really want and letting that guide you rather than being pushed around by the circumstances of life. It's like being the chef instead of just another diner waiting for whatever dish life serves up. And the best part? Manifestation makes life easier, because it helps you get clear on what you really want. Once you're clear, you can stop wasting energy on things that don't matter and start focusing on what does. It's like cleaning out your mental pantry, getting rid of the expired negativity, and stocking up on the ingredients that will help you cook up the life of your dreams.

A DASH OF HISTORY: WHERE DID MANIFESTATION COME FROM?

Manifestation isn't just some New Age buzzword that popped up with the rise of social media influencers and wellness gurus. Its roots run deep, all the way back to ancient civilizations that believed in the power of thoughts, words, and intentions to shape reality. From the Hermetic teachings in ancient Egypt, which professed that "the All is Mind," to the teachings of Hinduism and Buddhism about karma and the power of intention, the idea that our inner world shapes our outer world is an old one. It's like the spiritual equivalent of a family recipe passed down through generations. Fast-forward to the nineteenth century, and you have the New Thought movement, where folks like Phineas Quimby and Ralph Waldo Emerson started talking about the power of positive thinking. The idea simmered on the back burner for a while before making a big splash in the twenty-first century with the popularity of books like *The Secret.* Suddenly, everyone was talking about the Law of Attraction—the idea that positive or negative thoughts bring corresponding experiences into a person's life—as if it were the hottest new superfood.

THE SKEPTICS: THE CRITICS WHO SWEAR IT'S JUST A FLUFFY SOUFFLÉ

Now, not everyone's sold on the idea that you can think your way to a better life. Skeptics like to point out that just because you imagine yourself winning the lottery doesn't mean you'll actually hit the jackpot. They see manifestation as a fluffy soufflé—pretty to look at but lacking in substance. According to them, it's all wishful thinking, a mental placebo that only works because you've convinced yourself it will.

Life Lesson: Manifestation isn't about waving a magic wand and making your dream car appear in your driveway overnight. (I used to imagine this with my favorite foods, and poof, now we have Postmates.) It's about aligning your energy, thoughts, and actions with what you want to create in your life. It's about setting the stage in your mind so that the universe knows what kind of show you're trying to put on. When you consciously decide to focus on what you want rather than what you don't want, you're taking the reins of your life. You're choosing to believe in a world where your thoughts have power, and that belief is a game changer.

MANIFESTATION ACTIVATION CHALLENGE

So let's play. Choose something specific you'd like to bring into your life—something that feels achievable but still a bit beyond your current reach. Maybe it's a new job, a relationship, or a deeper sense of inner peace. Now that you're this far into the book, think beyond just creating a life of ease. What does that truly mean for you? Reflect back on your values from chapter 4. Which area of your life did you want to focus on, and what exactly do you want in that area that you don't already have?

Remember, manifesting isn't just about getting things; it's about embodying a feeling, a way of being. It's about becoming the person who can have, handle, and hold on to the things you desire. I've created a manifestation activation challenge to help you put your manifesting powers into action. Whether you complete it in full or use it as a gentle nudge when you need a metaphysical boost, approach this challenge in a way that feels authentic to you. (And a big thank you to the many who have come before me, whose recipes for manifestation helped shape this tasty treat.)

Welcome to your twenty-two-day journey into the heart of manifestation! This challenge is here to take you from daydreaming to real results. Remember, manifestation isn't just about getting the things you want. It's about embodying how you want to feel every single day. This challenge is designed to help you slide into authenticity and slip out of "shoulds."

Each day of this challenge is designed to help you become the person who effortlessly manifests your desires. As you go through it, you might notice things starting to shift— inside and out. Maybe you'll start seeing some of those tangible results you've been craving or even experience a few miracles along the way. There's no one-size-fits-all approach to this challenge. Just showing up is the "if you let it"; what unfolds is the "life gets to be easy." The results are uniquely yours. You can pull out this challenge anytime you're ready to manifest something new. (Just apply as needed, like that moisturizer you save for the lengthy skin-care days—but in this case, for your dreams!)

Think of this challenge as your daily recipe for success, where each day adds a new layer of flavor to the life you're cooking up. Try to dive into each challenge at the same time every day. Make it a ritual, a little ceremony. This regularity signals to your body that you're stepping into manifestation mode, and your brain will start to see it as a fun, exciting part of your day—not just another task on the to-do list.

Use the QR code to download the complete 22-Day Cosmic Concoction Manifestation Challenge workbook and audios to get the most hands-on and in-depth guidance and support while you manifest. Or use the following prompts and jot down what feels right! However you choose to do it, make it yours!

Ready to get started? Let's dive in.

THE 22-DAY COSMIC CONCOCTION MANIFESTATION CHALLENGE

DAY 1: WHAT'S ON THE MENU? DEFINE YOUR DESIRE

Start by getting crystal clear on what you want to manifest. This is your moment to dream big, so write down your desire in detail—make it specific, vivid, and exciting.

DAY 2: TASTE IT BEFORE IT'S COOKED— VISUALIZE YOUR SUCCESS

Close your eyes and spend ten minutes visualizing your desire as if it's already real. Picture the details—what you're wearing, where you are, and how it feels to have what you've been dreaming of. Engage all your senses, making this mental movie as vivid as possible. This daily practice stirs up excitement and anticipation, priming your mind to bring your vision to life.

DAY 3: STIR THE POT—SHIFT YOUR ENERGY

Today's task is about keeping your vibe high. Pay attention to your thoughts, and if you catch yourself slipping into negativity, pause. It's like catching a burning smell before it ruins the dish—don't let those thoughts overcook! Flip negative thoughts into positive ones, like swapping out a sour ingredient for something sweet.

DAY 4: START COOKING—TAKE ALIGNED ACTION

Manifestation is teamwork between you and the universe. Today, roll up your sleeves and take a small, inspired action that moves you closer to your goal. Whether it's updating your résumé or going for a walk, each step signals to the universe that you're serious about your desires. Experiment with something you've been avoiding. You don't need to perfect it—just try. How does it feel?

DAY 5: SEASON WITH LOVE—CULTIVATE GRATITUDE

Write down ten things you're grateful for, including one related to your desire, as if it's already yours. Gratitude shifts your focus to what's already amazing, attracting more goodness.

DAY 6: LET IT SIMMER—RELEASE RESISTANCE

Identify any resistance toward your desire and imagine releasing it, like letting go of old ingredients you no longer need. If letting go is hard, place your hand on your heart and affirm, "I release what no longer serves me."

DAY 7: SET IT ON LOW HEAT—ANCHOR YOUR FAITH

Create a daily affirmation that resonates with you, and repeat it throughout the day to keep your faith strong and aligned. To make it more effective, pair your affirmation with a physical action, like placing your hand on your heart.

DAY 8: CONSULT THE CHEF—CONNECT WITH YOUR HIGHER SELF

Spend ten minutes in meditation or quiet reflection, asking your higher self for guidance. What do you need to know today to stay aligned with your desire? Listen to the wisdom that comes through, and then act on it. Journal your insights—this will help you stay in tune with your inner guidance.

DAY 9: PRACTICE PLATING—STEP INTO IT

Embody the energy of your desires as if they're already real. Dress, act, and carry yourself like the person you want to be. Curate your surroundings to reflect the life you're manifesting, like creating a workspace that inspires success.

DAY 10: ADD A SURPRISE INGREDIENT— EMBRACE THE UNEXPECTED

Today's all about being open to the surprises life throws

your way. Stay alert and pay close attention to the people, situations, or ideas that cross your path. These surprises are often the universe's way of delivering something even better than what you initially asked for. When something unexpected happens today, instead of reacting out of habit, pause to consider how it might be aligned with what you're manifesting. Ask yourself, *How could this be serving my highest good?*

DAY 11: SLOW-COOK FOR MAXIMUM FLAVOR—PRACTICE PATIENCE

Manifestation is like a slow-cooked meal—it takes time to reach its full, delicious potential. Today, your challenge is to practice patience and trust in the timing of your desire. Remember, just because you don't see immediate results doesn't mean things aren't simmering away behind the scenes. Take a moment to reflect on a time when patience really paid off in your life.

DAY 12: TASTE TEST—REVISIT YOUR VISION

Today is all about checking in and making sure your manifestation is still on track. Think of it as a taste test—sampling your vision to see if it's coming together just the way you imagined. Check in with your original intention. Does it still excite you? If something feels off, refine your vision.

DAY 13: TURN UP THE HEAT—AMPLIFY YOUR VIBRATION

Today is all about raising your energy and boosting your vibration—because the higher your vibe, the faster your manifestations can take shape. Have some fun, play, and embrace joy! Engage in activities that lift your spirits and raise your vibration, like dancing, spending time in nature, or laughing with friends. Create a "High-Vibe Toolkit" of activities, music, and quotes that instantly lift your mood.

DAY 14: SPICE IT UP—CRANK UP THE CREATIVITY

While day 13 focused on uplifting your energy through joy and movement, today is about tapping into your creative essence. Creativity opens doors to new ideas and possibilities. Try something new, reconnect with old passions, or try creative problem-solving. Embrace the unexpected in your creativity without worrying about the outcome—let it flow.

DAY 15: THE UNIVERSE'S TASTE TEST— CHECK FOR SIGNS

This one is my favorite! Today is all about paying attention to the signs that the universe is sending your way, signaling that your manifestation is unfolding. These signs are like little nudges from the universe, reassuring you that you're on the right path and that your desires are in progress. Take note of the messages guiding you. Choose a meaningful sign, and let go of control. Trust the process.

DAY 16: ENJOY THE APPETIZERS—CELEBRATE SMALL WINS

Acknowledge and celebrate small achievements along your manifestation journey. They keep you motivated and attract more success. Create a "Small Wins Jar" to collect positive milestones and review them when you need a boost.

DAY 17: SET THE TABLE—CLEAR YOUR SPACE

Today's focus is on creating a physical environment that welcomes new energy and supports your manifestations. Unlike day 9, when you might have arranged your space to reflect the life you're stepping into, this step is about clearing out the old to make room for the new. After decluttering, smudge your space or light a candle to clear any stagnant energy.

DAY 18: INVITE OTHERS TO THE TABLE— SHARE YOUR VISION

Today is all about amplifying the energy of your manifestation by sharing your goals and desires with someone you trust. When you openly discuss your vision, you not only strengthen your commitment to it but also invite support and encouragement from the universe through the people around you. To make the most of this practice, ask the person you share with if they have any resources, connections, or experiences that might help you on your journey.

DAY 19: ADD A DASH OF DETERMINATION— REAFFIRM YOUR COMMITMENT

Today is about renewing your commitment to your manifestation with fresh energy and focus. Recommit to your goals by writing down three specific actions you'll take in the next week, which will keep your momentum strong. Set reminders for each action to stay on track, and celebrate each step forward.

DAY 20: STEP OUT OF THE KITCHEN— RELEASE CONTROL

Today, it's time to step out of the kitchen and trust that your manifestation is cooking to perfection. You've done the prep work and added all the right ingredients, and now it's time to let the dish finish on its own. This step is all about releasing control and allowing the universe to handle the rest. Engage in an activity that takes your mind off the process, like spending time with loved ones or enjoying a hobby.

DAY 21: TASTE AND ADJUST—REFLECT AND REFINE

Today is all about taking a step back and reflecting on the journey you've been on over the past twenty days. Think of it as tasting the dish you've been carefully preparing— what flavors have developed, and how has the process shaped you? Reflect on your journey and adjust your manifestation practice based on what you've learned. Create a "Manifestation Recipe Card" with the most effective strategies from the challenge for future reference.

DAY 22: ENJOY THE FEAST—CELEBRATE YOUR JOURNEY

Congratulations on completing the whole manifestation challenge! It's time to celebrate the journey you've taken and the growth you've achieved. Whether your manifestation has fully arrived or is still on its way, honor your progress and keep the momentum going. If you're ready to dive deeper, a more detailed version of this challenge is available on my website, offering extra tools and guidance. Plus, with the book's QR code, you get the best price! This is just the beginning of a lifetime of delicious manifestations. WOO-HOO! I AM SO PROUD OF YOU!

GRATITUDE: THE ART OF ABUNDANCE

As we close this chapter on spirituality, it's no accident that we're ending with gratitude. This isn't just the last lesson; it's the lesson that ties everything together. Gratitude is the thread that runs through all spiritual practices, weaving together the insights, experiences, and growth you've gained. It's what allows you to truly let life be easy. When you're grateful, you're not fighting against life; you're flowing with it. Gratitude is a concept that pops up in nearly every spiritual practice for a reason. It's not just a nice-to-have; it's a game changer. Across cultures and belief systems, from ancient teachings to modern self-help books, gratitude is held up as one of the most powerful forces you can harness in your life. But why is that? What makes gratitude such a universal cornerstone of spiritual practice?

At its core, gratitude is about shifting your perspective. It's about choosing to focus on what's going right instead of fixating on what's wrong. And this simple shift has a profound impact on how you experience the world. When you start to see life through the lens of gratitude, everything changes. The mundane becomes magical, the challenges become opportunities, and the ordinary becomes extraordinary. Gratitude isn't just a fleeting feeling—it's a way of being. It's a practice that roots you firmly in the present moment, helping you to appreciate the here and now rather than constantly longing for what's next.

In a world that's always pushing us to want more, do more, and be more, gratitude invites us to pause, breathe, and recognize that we already have enough. It teaches us that abundance isn't something to be chased; it's something to be acknowledged and appreciated in the present moment. And this is where the real magic happens. When you live in a state of gratitude, you're not just changing your own mindset—you're actually shifting the energy you release into the world. You begin to notice more opportunities, more joy, and more connections that align with your true self.

But the importance of gratitude goes even deeper. It's a practice that aligns you with the flow of life, helping you to let go of resistance and embrace what is. In many spiritual traditions, gratitude is seen as the antidote to fear, anger, and resentment. It's the practice that softens your heart and opens you up to the beauty and possibilities that surround you every day. Gratitude also connects you to something greater than yourself. Whether you see it as connecting to the divine, the universe, or simply the collective energy of humanity, gratitude reminds you that you are part of a larger whole. It's a practice that grounds you, reminding you that you're supported, guided, and loved—no matter what challenges you face.

Think of mind, body, and spirit as your personal dream team, working behind the scenes to keep your life in harmony. And gratitude? Gratitude is the coach, the unsung hero that makes sure everyone's playing nicely together. When you practice gratitude, you're not just doing a good deed—you're recalibrating your entire existence. You're saying, "Hey, universe, I see the good stuff, and I'm ready for more." And the universe, being the generous friend it is, says, "Oh, you like that? Here, have some extra!" Without gratitude, it's like trying to bake a cake without sugar—not impossible, but definitely not as sweet. Gratitude isn't just a practice; it's the heartbeat of a life that's easy, fulfilling, and unapologetically yours. Keep counting those blessings, because they're the breadcrumbs that lead you to a life that's both easy and absolutely delicious.

COOKING WITH CLARITY

Alright, let's get real for a second. We've covered a lot of ground in this chapter, diving into the deep end of spirituality and discovering how it all ties back to living a life of ease. But heed my suggestion: mind, body, and spirit aren't just abstract concepts you read about and forget. They're the triple threat that makes everything flow smoothly. These are the life lessons we should have learned ages ago, but hey, better late than never, right? Up to this point in the book, you've been carefully crafting a hearty dish—a life that feels more aligned, more intentional, and yes, a little easier. You've gathered the essential ingredients, mixed them together with care, and let them simmer into something truly nourishing. Mind, body, spirit—they've all played their part, and with gratitude as the mouthwatering seasoning, you've created something rich and fulfilling. But before you're ready to serve this dish to the world, it's time to get clear on the vision of the life you want to live. Welcome to your clarity compass.

PART 3

THE ALCHEMY OF AUTHENTICITY

Master the art of shifting your
perspective and steering it toward ease.

CHAPTER 7

YOUR CLARITY COMPASS

"If you are working on something exciting that you really care about, you don't have to be pushed. The vision pulls you."

—Steve Jobs

INTRODUCTION TO CLARITY

Isn't life easier with clarity? Life without clarity is like running a marathon without knowing where the finish line is. It's exhausting and directionless, and you're likely to end up more frustrated than fulfilled. But when you have clarity—when you know what you truly want and what to do to attract it—every step feels more like a purposeful stride and less like a frantic sprint. Clarity is your compass; it points you toward a life of ease and fulfillment. It's about understanding your deepest desires, recognizing your core values, and aligning your actions with your purpose.

So why does clarity come in chapter 7? Why not dive into it right from the start? Here's the thing: clarity isn't something you can just snap your fingers and find. It's like baking a cake—you can't frost it before it's fully baked. In the first few chapters, we laid the groundwork. We explored your deeper desires, uncovered the blocks standing in your way, and embraced the investments that support awareness and acceptance. We dug into your why, that driving force behind your desire for change. But without clarity, all those insights are just ingredients waiting to be mixed.

Now that you've done the heavy lifting—moving the roadblocks aside, deciding to invest in yourself, and accepting that change is not just needed but wanted—you're ready to let your values and vision flourish. Clarity is the ingredient that turns your intention into action and your dreams into plans. By focusing on clarity now, you're setting the stage for everything that follows. It's the moment when the fog lifts. You can see the path ahead with fresh eyes, and you're ready to walk it with purpose and confidence. This is where your values and vision become not just ideas but the very foundation of your life.

As Steve Jobs said above, "If you are working on something exciting that you really care about, you don't have to be pushed. The vision pulls you." And that's the power of clarity: it transforms your journey into one where you're naturally drawn toward your dreams, guided by your vision and values. This chapter breaks down the elements of your clarity compass and how to use it effectively when discovering and navigating toward your authentic purpose.

THE VISION QUEST

Let's dive into a little exercise I like to call a "vision quest." Don't worry; you won't need to trek through the desert or fast for days (unless that's your thing). This is about visualizing your ideal day, the kind of day where everything feels just right. This is a visualization of your most authentic self. If your Passion Pledge involves something specific, like a higher-paying job or a more fulfilling relationship, visualize a day in the life of already having those things.

Be as specific as you possibly can. In the process of manifesting what you want, the more specific you are about your desires and vision for your life, the stronger your connection will be as you get closer to achieving them. You'll recognize what success feels like in relation to your desires because you've already visualized and embodied the emotions that achieving your goals will bring. This isn't just about the activities you choose but also about how they make you feel. Close your eyes and imagine your perfect day, and then write down what you see on a piece of paper or in your journal:

→ What does your morning look like? Are you sipping coffee on a sun-drenched balcony, or are you hitting the ground running with a workout? How do you feel when you start your day? Are you energized, peaceful, or inspired? Picture yourself in that state.

→ How do you spend your afternoon? How do the activities you engage in—whether it's creative work, collaboration, or exploration—make you feel? Fulfilled, connected, or curious?

→ What's your evening like? Are you winding down with a good book, enjoying a meal with loved ones, or reflecting on your day with a sense of accomplishment? As you wind down, what emotions are present? Are you content, proud, or reflective?

Focus on the feelings, experiences, and activities that bring you genuine joy and fulfillment. This isn't about what you think you should want but about what truly lights you up. When you have a vision that excites you, the path to realizing it becomes clearer and more accessible because you understand how you want to feel. Even if you don't know exactly how to achieve your vision or what steps to take, you've already begun to familiarize yourself with the feeling of that vision. The feelings behind the activities help guide you in the right direction. Like tuning in to a radio station, once you find the right frequency, the music comes through loud and clear.

CORE VALUES: YOUR PERSONAL NORTH STAR

Now that you have in mind a vision of the life you want, let's talk about core values. They are the fundamental beliefs that guide our behavior and decision-making. They are deeply ingrained and shape our understanding of what is important in life. They're the nonnegotiables, the things you won't compromise on because they're essential to who you are. When I work with a client, it's not uncommon to spend months clarifying and landing on the core values that feel most important. I offer this sentiment because I want to dispel the notion that these values are a fixed component in your life. They may change and evolve, as anything will.

Here's the thing: our brains aren't exactly designed to juggle a million things at once (even if we often try to). According to Cognitive Load Theory, our working memory is like that overstuffed junk drawer we all have—it can only hold so much before it starts to get chaotic. So, when it comes to your core values, it's best to keep them simple and streamlined.

This might come as a surprise (and maybe even a relief), but despite feeling like we're a walking cocktail of values, most of us can only effectively manage around five core values at any given time. Yep, just five. Think of it like carrying a handful of marbles—add too many, and they start slipping through your fingers, leading to confusion and stress.

Focusing on just five core values isn't some strict psychological rule but a practical approach that helps keep your sanity intact. Too many priorities can make life feel like a game of Twister, where you're stretching yourself in every direction and not really getting anywhere. But when you narrow down to a few key values, you're better equipped to align your actions with what truly matters to you.

Consider these core values your North Star in the clarity compass—guiding you toward the life you want to create without getting lost in the noise. When you know what your top values are, you're more likely to stay on track toward your goals. Not only that, but your core values will reveal when something is out of alignment in your life, offering you the opportunity to change. With fewer values to juggle, you'll find it easier to make decisions that reflect who you are at your core. (And let's be honest, you wanted life to be easier, right?)

DEFINING YOUR CORE VALUES

Take a moment to really think about what drives you at your core. What are the nonnegotiables, the guiding principles that keep you grounded and true to yourself? These are your core values. Maybe yours are honesty, creativity, connection, integrity, and joy. Whatever they are, write them down and let them sink in. Notice if your values appeared in your vision quest. They're like the islands in the movie *Inside Out*—they shape who you are and influence every decision you make.

For example, if one of your core values is creativity, you might feel suffocated in a job that stifles your creative expression. It's like living in a world where your "Creativity Island" is crumbling, leaving you feeling disconnected and out of sync with yourself. But when you align your work with this value—whether that's by starting your own business, pursuing a creative hobby, or even just finding ways to be more innovative in your current role—you'll find yourself feeling more fulfilled, more at ease, and more connected to your purpose.

If you value freedom, like I do, you might struggle with rigid schedules or environments that limit your autonomy. For me, freedom is about having the flexibility to choose how I spend my time, the ability to explore new ideas and opportunities, and the space to grow without being confined by others' expectations. This value shows up in my career choices, in the way I structure my day, and even in the relationships I cultivate. I need room to breathe, to move, and to express myself fully—otherwise, I start to feel trapped and stagnant (which is not my vision of the life I desire!).

Authentic expression is another big one for me. Whether it's through writing, speaking, or even just how I dress, I need to be able to express who I am authentically. If I'm in a situation where I feel like I have to mute my voice or hide parts of myself, it's like my "Expression Island" is under attack, and I'm left feeling unfulfilled and disconnected. But when I'm free to express myself, I feel more alive, more aligned, and more at ease.

Service and self-development are also central to who I am. I find deep fulfillment in helping others and in continually growing and evolving as a person. These values guide me in my career as a life coach, in the way I show up for my friends and family, and in the goals I set for myself. When I'm in alignment with these values, I'm not just existing— I'm thriving.

And then there's truth. If my values are my North Star, truth is the wavelength of light that is most illuminating when I feel lost; it is my grounding force. I strive to be honest with myself and others, even when it's uncomfortable. Living in alignment with truth means that I'm constantly checking in with myself, making sure that my actions and decisions reflect my true feelings and beliefs. It's about cutting through the noise and the expectations of others to get to the heart of what really matters to me.

So, take a moment to identify your own core values. Maybe you value security, adventure, kindness, or authenticity. Whatever they are, these values constitute the islands that shape your world. They influence how you think, feel, and act. If your Passion Pledge is the destination, your values are the true north that establishes all the other compass directions, and your vision is the gravitational pull that points your needle in the right direction. When you align your actions with these values, life feels more effortless, more meaningful, and yes, easier.

And if you're still not sure what your values are, think about the moments when you've felt most alive, most at peace, or most proud of yourself. What was happening in those moments? What were you doing? How were you showing up? The answers to these questions will give you clues about what truly matters to you. Once you've identified your values, you'll start to see how they influence every aspect of your life—from your career choices to your relationships to how you spend your free time. It's all connected, and when you live in alignment with your values, everything just starts to click into place.

PURPOSE: YOUR CLARITY COMPASS

Purpose is essential because it gives you a reason to get up in the morning, as well as a sense of direction that keeps you moving forward even when the seas get rough. It's the keel that keeps you upright and the wind that fills your sails. Without purpose, it's easy to feel like you're just going through the motions, living a life that doesn't quite fit. There's a lot of pressure in our culture to "find your purpose," and it can feel overwhelming if you're not sure what that is. But here's the thing: purpose doesn't have to be some grand, world-changing mission.

I want to share a tool that can help you define your purpose in tangible ways by connecting the dots between what you love, what you're good at, and where you want to make an impact. It's about recognizing the areas in your life that feel disconnected or unfulfilling and taking actionable steps to bring more of your core values into those spaces. By doing so, you'll not only clarify your purpose but also start living more authentically in a way that feels true and meaningful to you.

The clarity compass is an exercise designed to help you navigate through the fog of uncertainty and steer you toward a life that feels aligned with who you are at your core. By guiding you through a series of thoughtful questions, this tool helps you pinpoint areas of your life where you might be out of alignment with your true self. It's a practical approach to identifying where your purpose might be lacking or where you're not fully living in accordance with your values. Ready to chart your course? Let's set sail and discover the life you were meant to live. (We've gone from stirring the pot to steering the ship, folks. The analogy game is strong; keep up!)

USING YOUR CLARITY COMPASS

Whenever you feel out of alignment with the vision of the life you want to live (or your Passion Pledge), answer the following questions.

STEP 1: Hoist Your Sail

What do you love in life? Think about the passions and interests that naturally energize you and light you up. Start by listing out everything that sparks joy and happiness— don't worry about the number. It could be three things, or it could be thirty. There's no right or wrong here. The key is to recognize what truly excites you. If you find yourself overwhelmed or struggling to narrow it down, try focusing on the top five to ten that resonate most deeply. This is about quality, not quantity.

If you're unsure, start by pinpointing what causes you to drift off course. Then, flip those distractions to reveal the true wind that should be filling your sails. For example, if you dread routine tasks, perhaps you're driven by creativity and spontaneity.

STEP 2: Check Your Compass

What are the skills and talents that keep your ship on course? What are you good at? These are your compass points—the unique abilities that help you navigate through

rough waters with ease. Consider what people praise you for or the tasks you perform effortlessly.

For example, are you the one everyone turns to for advice or problem-solving? That's a sign your compass is set toward leadership or innovation.

STEP 3: UNLOCK YOUR SHORTCUT

Now that you've hoisted your sail and calibrated your compass, it's time to unveil your hidden shortcut—your personal GPS to success. This is where your passions and skills intersect, creating a sweet spot of expertise that not only sets you apart but also makes the journey smoother and more enjoyable. When you operate in your zone of genius (or, as I like to call it, your "shortcut to awesome"), you're not just working harder—you're working smarter. You're tapping into a flow state where things just click, and progress feels almost effortless.

Hint: If you find yourself constantly drawn to certain activities, or if people regularly seek your advice on specific topics, congratulations—you've likely stumbled upon your shortcut. Imagine it as finding a secret passage in a maze; while everyone else is still wandering around, you're breezing through, getting closer to your destination with each step because you have a special power that propels you forward.

STEP 4: IDENTIFY YOUR NORTH STAR

What are the core values that guide you, like the North Star guiding a ship at night? These values are the unwavering points that keep you on the right course, no matter how turbulent the waters become. For example, my core values are freedom, authentic expression, service, self-development, and truth. These values illuminate my path and guide every decision, big or small.

STEP 5: SURVEY THE HORIZON

Examine the different areas of your life—your career, relationships, personal growth, and so on. Which one feels like you're adrift or caught in a storm? Pinpoint the area that needs a course correction. For instance, if your relationship feels unfulfilling, it's time to adjust your sails and realign your compass to get back on track.

STEP 6: ADJUST YOUR SAILS

Take a closer look at your top five values—are any of them being neglected in the area you've chosen to focus on? If you're feeling out of sync, it's likely because one of these core values isn't getting the attention it deserves. If, for example, connection is a top value for you, but your relationship has been stuck in surface-level conversations and routine check-ins, it's time to course-correct. Maybe you need to steer your relationship toward deeper, more meaningful interactions, like setting aside time for heartfelt talks or shared activities that bring you closer.

STEP 7: CATCH THE WIND AND SET SAIL

Now that you've identified the value that's missing in your life, it's time to catch the wind and set your course toward a more fulfilling path. Instead of overhauling everything at once, start by experimenting with small actions that can bring that value back into focus. What's one specific action you can try this week? Whether it's dedicating time to a neglected hobby, making time for self-care, or initiating a meaningful conversation, the goal isn't perfection—it's about getting comfortable with experimenting. So, catch the wind, set sail, and see where this new journey takes you.

To continue the previous example, if connection is what's lacking, think about simple ways to bridge that gap. Maybe it's planning an impromptu date night or just taking a few minutes each day to check in with your partner in a meaningful way. The key here is not to stress about getting it perfect—this is about dipping your toes in and seeing what feels right.

Life is a journey, and your clarity compass is there to help you navigate it. The path to purpose isn't always a straight line, but with your compass in hand, you can adjust your course as needed. Each decision and action brings you a step closer to the life you're meant to live—one filled with purpose, ease, and authenticity. It doesn't have to be a stormy voyage; with the right tools, smooth sailing is entirely possible. But before we hoist the sails and catch the wind, let's unpack the idea of letting your vision pull you forward, like a gentle current guiding your course so that you don't have to fight the tide.

INTRINSIC VS. EXTRINSIC MOTIVATION: THE WIND IN YOUR SAILS

When you know what really drives you—whether it's the joy from within or the approval from outside—you can steer your life in a way that feels less like rowing against the current. Understanding these concepts is like fine-tuning your compass, making sure you're headed in the right direction for a life that feels genuinely fulfilling, not just like you're ticking off boxes. It's almost as if there's a reason they didn't emphasize these ideas in school—because if we all knew why we did things, we might just have a better sense of authenticity from the start (and that kind of power scares people).

Intrinsic motivation is that internal spark that drives you to do something simply because you love it or find it meaningful. It's the joy you feel when you're painting, writing, or playing a sport—not for a prize or recognition but because the activity itself is fulfilling. Intrinsic motivation is like the rich, homemade broth in a soup—it's nourishing, comforting, and satisfying all on its own. It doesn't need anything extra to make it worthwhile.

On the other hand, *extrinsic motivation* is fueled by external rewards or pressures. You might be driven to work late hours because of a looming deadline or the promise of a bonus. It's the motivation that comes from outside yourself, like adding a splash of store-bought stock to your soup because you're out of time or ingredients. It'll do the job, but it doesn't have the same depth or richness as something that comes from within.

Life Lesson: Life feels easier when it's driven by intrinsic motivation. When you're motivated by what genuinely excites and fulfills you, the effort you put in doesn't feel like work. It feels like play, passion, or purpose. You're more resilient, more creative, and less likely to burn out. While extrinsic motivation has its place, it will often leave you feeling depleted if it's your main source of fuel. It's like running on fumes—you might get where you need to go, but it won't necessarily be a pleasant journey.

INNER CRITIC VS. JOY: THE BATTLE FOR YOUR ATTENTION

Now, let's talk about the inner critic and joy—two opposing forces that like to hang out in the motivation zone, each with plenty to say. I don't like to live in dichotomies, so let's refrain from labeling either of these energies as good or bad. They both serve their purpose in our survival, and both think they're the spoon that stirs the soup. (Before we all start reaching for the Dramamine, I'm going to retire the sailing analogy—for now.)

Your inner critic is that nagging voice that tells you that you're not good enough, that you're going to fail, or that you're not doing as well as you should be. It's the equivalent of adding a bitter herb to your otherwise perfect recipe— it leaves a bad taste, dampening your enthusiasm and making the whole process feel arduous. The inner critic feeds off extrinsic motivation, constantly pushing you to meet external standards and punishing you when you don't.

But with all things, that inner critic, as annoying as it can be, isn't entirely useless. Sometimes, it pushes you out of your comfort zone, urging you to strive for more. It's like that one ingredient in the pantry that you are hesitant to use but know can elevate a dish if incorporated correctly. The problem is the inner critic often oversteps, turning what could be a gentle nudge into a relentless shove. While it can spur growth, it can also make the journey feel a lot harder than it needs to be.

Joy, on the other hand, is the sweet ingredient that makes life delicious. It's the feeling you get when you're doing something that lights you up, like dancing around your kitchen while making dinner or losing yourself in a good book. Joy is what happens when you're driven by intrinsic motivation—it's the reward that comes from the act itself, not from external validation. When joy is leading the way, everything feels easier, lighter, and more fun. The effort doesn't feel like effort at all; it feels like flow, like you're in sync with the rhythm of your life.

But remember that ease is not the absence of effort! Joy isn't just about playing around and avoiding work. It's deeply linked to authenticity. When you truly know yourself, you can identify what brings you joy and leverage it to create meaningful results. Joy is an indicator that you're on the right path, doing something that not only excites you but also expands you. It's like finding the perfect balance of flavors in a dish; everything just clicks.

When you're connected to your authentic self, joy becomes your guide, showing you where to invest your energy. It's about enjoying the process because you can feel that it's not just about the outcome—it's about the growth and fulfillment you experience along the way. Joy tells you that you're aligned with your values and that what you're doing is not just another to-do list item but something that resonates with who you truly are. It's the fuel that keeps you moving forward, making the journey feel less like a chore and more like an adventure.

THE CONNECTION TO EASE

So how does all this tie back to the idea that life gets to be easy if you let it? The key is recognizing which force is driving you—your inner critic or joy, extrinsic or intrinsic motivation. When you let joy and intrinsic motivation take the lead, you align yourself with activities, people, and goals that resonate with your true self. You're not constantly striving to meet someone else's standards or chasing external rewards. Instead, you're driven by what genuinely matters to you, which naturally brings a sense of ease into your life. Imagine waking up every day excited about what's ahead because you're doing things that make you feel alive and fulfilled. That's the power of intrinsic motivation and joy—they make the hard things feel easier, and the easy things feel like pure magic.

But there's one more thing you need to add: your special sauce. This is where everything comes together, where the flavors deepen, and your unique touch transforms a good dish into something unforgettable. The art of authenticity is the final ingredient, the one that makes your life unmistakably yours. It's what elevates everything you've done so far, taking it from something hearty and comforting to something that truly stands out.

As we move forward, get ready to discover what makes you *you*. Because this dish isn't complete until you've added your special sauce—your true self, fully expressed. That's when the magic happens: your life becomes a reflection of who you really are, and you're ready to share it with the world. So, grab your compass, and let's stir up your special sauce.

CHAPTER 8

YOUR SPECIAL SAUCE

*"Anyone can cook, but only the
fearless can be great."*

—Chef Gusteau, Ratatouille

(I had to.)

EMBRACING YOUR UNIQUE FLAVOR

Until now, we've focused on the foundational work of letting life be easy, using your clarity compass to steer you in the direction of your desires, and learning to flow with the rhythms of mind, body, and spirit. But now, we're bottling up the essence of everything you've crafted, labeling it with your unique stamp, and uncovering the secret ingredient that makes it unmistakably yours. This is the step where you take all those carefully selected ingredients, blend them into something distinctly you, and package it as your signature flavor—ready to share with the world in all its authentic glory.

This is where you start whipping up your special sauce—the one that makes you stand out in a sea of similar ingredients. Just like Chef Gusteau says in *Ratatouille*, "Anyone can cook, but only the fearless can be great." (And yes, I'm dropping quotes from philosophers and musicians throughout this book, but I'm definitely not above referencing Pixar—those geniuses totally get it!) The same goes for life: anyone can go through the motions, but it's the ones who are brave enough to live authentically, to embrace their unique flavor, who create something truly extraordinary.

In this chapter, we're going to explore what makes you you. This is about more than just understanding your values and goals—it's about digging deeper to find the magic blend that defines your essence. Everyone has access to the same basic ingredients, but what sets you apart is how you mix them, how you season them, and how you serve them up to the world. It's the way you move through life, the impact you have on others, and the energy you carry. Your special sauce is that magic mix of qualities that, when fully realized, makes you irresistible and unforgettable.

Life Lesson: Discovering this sauce isn't about copying someone else's recipe. It's about exploring what's already within you, embracing the unique combination of experiences, strengths, and quirks that only you possess. In a world where we're often tempted to conform, your special sauce is what keeps you authentic, vibrant, and unapologetically *you*.

DISCOVERING YOUR ESSENCE

So, what really makes you *you*? This question is like peeling back the layers of an onion—there's always more beneath the surface, and sometimes it brings tears to your eyes. It's a question that dives deep, going beyond simple labels and definitions. This isn't just about slapping a few adjectives on your personality and calling it a day. No, this is about the impression you leave in your wake, the inspiration you spark in others, and the connections you weave that last long after the moment has passed.

Think of it as your signature taste—the lingering flavor that sticks around long after the meal is over, making people say, "Wow, that was something special." **Life Lesson:** Discovering your essence isn't as straightforward as following a recipe. It's not something you can neatly package up and present on a silver platter. It's fluid and ever changing, like a sauce that evolves with every new ingredient you toss in and every experience you let simmer.

Start by asking yourself some real, introspective questions. What do people say about you when you're not in the room? How do you want to be remembered when all is said and done? These aren't just idle musings—they're the first steps to uncovering the core of your special sauce. But remember, your essence isn't just about how others perceive you; it's also deeply tied to how you see yourself.

Discovering your essence can feel like trying to catch lightning in a bottle. It's elusive, often slipping through your fingers just when you think you've got it figured out. It's the kind of thing that's hard to measure because it's not about fitting into predefined categories. It's a feeling, an energy, a vibe that you carry with you wherever you go. Narrowing down your essence can feel like trying to fit the ocean into a teacup. It's expansive and multifaceted, and it can't be fully captured in a few words. And that's okay.

Your essence isn't static; it's dynamic and evolves with you as you grow and change. This phase is where you need to get comfortable with a bit of ambiguity. It's not about finding a definitive answer that will stick with you forever—it's about exploring, playing with different ideas, and seeing what resonates with you right now. Your essence might be clearer in some areas of your life than others, and that's part of the journey.

Life Lesson: These questions are not always easy to confront. This may be the first time you've ever really stopped to think about your essence, and that can be challenging and even a bit uncomfortable. But the process of discovering your essence yields magic. It's about stripping away the expectations, letting go of the narratives thrust upon you or that you've adopted for yourself, and retiring all the other *bullshit*. It's about digging deep, confronting the parts of yourself that you might have kept hidden or ignored, and bringing them into the light.

Think of your essence as the awe-inspiring ingredient in a complex dish. It's not the obvious flavor that hits you first but the subtle undertone that gives the dish its depth and character. It's the way you laugh, the way you listen, and the way you make people feel understood. It's the choices you make when no one's watching and the dreams you chase, even when they seem out of reach.

Maybe your essence is in the way you bring people together. You're the glue in your friend group, the one who makes sure everyone feels included and valued. It's not something you consciously try to do—it's just who you are. Or perhaps your essence shows up in the way you tackle challenges head-on, with a mix of resilience and optimism that inspires others to keep going even when the going gets tough.

But essence isn't always about the big, bold gestures. It's often found in the quiet moments too. Maybe it's the way you approach your work with a meticulous eye for detail or how you take the time to really listen to someone when they need to be heard. It's the little things that often go unnoticed but make a world of difference. If you're having trouble owning your greatness, let me help you out.

WHO DO YOU ADMIRE, AND WHY?

Think about the people who make you stop and say, "Wow, they've got something special." It could be anyone—a friend, a family member, a public figure, or even a character from a book or movie. There's a reason these people catch your attention, and it's more than just admiration from afar. (I love Taylor Swift and praise her for her empire, but my admiration vote goes to the Jo Marches, Elizabeth Gilberts, and the Simone Bileses of the world, and I'll reveal why in a minute!)

Life Lesson: Often, the traits we look up to in others are a reflection of qualities we either already possess or are yearning to develop within ourselves. It's like seeing a part of your potential come to life in someone else, giving you a glimpse of what's possible for you too. Think about it: if you admire someone's courage, it's likely because you value bravery in yourself. Maybe you've faced challenges that required you to dig deep and find your own courage, or maybe you're on the brink of a big decision where courage is exactly what you need. When you're drawn to someone's creativity, it could be a clue that there's a wellspring of imagination and innovation within you waiting to be tapped into. Admiring someone's relentless pursuit of their goals might reflect your own drive and determination, qualities that perhaps you've only just begun to embrace.

These reflections are like a mirror, showing you the aspects of yourself that resonate on a deep, soulful level. They're key ingredients in your special sauce, waiting to be blended into the unique flavor that is you. When you see someone else embodying a quality you admire, it's a signal from your inner self saying, *Hey, this is something I care about too.* **Life Lesson:** Admiration isn't about comparison. It's not about measuring yourself against someone else's yardstick or feeling like you're falling short. Instead, it's about recognizing the resonance. It's about understanding that the qualities you admire in others are often the very same ones that make you shine. They're the breadcrumbs—wait, no, we're done with breadcrumbs—they're the clues revealing to you the parts of yourself that are ripe for growth and expression.

So, how do you take this admiration and turn it into something actionable, something that adds to your special sauce? First, acknowledge that these qualities are already within you. Maybe they're still in the developmental phase, or maybe they've been a part of you all along, quietly influencing your choices and interactions. Either way, it's time to own them. For instance, if you admire someone's kindness, take a moment to reflect on how compassion shows up in your own life. Are you the one who always checks in on friends when they're going through a tough time? Do you find yourself going out of your way to make others feel comfortable and included? That's compassion in action, and it's a big part of who you are.

If you're drawn to someone's creativity, ask yourself how you express your own creative energy. Maybe it's through art, writing, problem-solving, or even the way you approach everyday tasks with a fresh perspective. Creativity isn't limited to being an artist—it's about seeing the world in a way that's uniquely yours and finding innovative ways to bring your ideas to life. And if it's tenacity that you admire, think about the times you've pushed through obstacles, refused to give up, or stayed committed to a goal even when the going got tough. Tenacity is more than just sticking it out—it's about believing in your own ability to overcome, no matter the challenges you face.

Alright, I'll spill why my admiration goes to the Jo Marches, Elizabeth Gilberts, and Simone Bileses of the world. These women are the real deal—they're fierce and unapologetically themselves, and they've got a kind of resilience that makes you want to stand up and cheer. And if I'm being humbly honest? I feel that about myself! I own it! Jo March isn't just a character in a book (*Little Women* by Louisa May Alcott, which is a must-read, and I highly recommend both modern film adaptations); she's a symbol of living life on your own terms, no matter what society expects. She's the original "do you" kind of woman, refusing to be boxed in by anyone else's idea of who she should be. With her defiance of societal expectations and relentless pursuit of her dreams, Jo March reminds me that staying true to oneself is a radical act of courage.

Then there's Elizabeth Gilbert (the "go find yourself and write about it" guru, author of *Eat, Pray, Love* and *Big Magic*), who not only went on a wild journey of self-discovery but also had the guts to share it with the world. She reminds us that vulnerability isn't a weakness—it's a superpower that can lead to the most incredible transformations and is as valuable as the destination.

And let's not forget Simone Biles. She didn't just dominate gymnastics—she redefined greatness by showing us that true strength includes knowing when to step back. When she prioritized her mental health, even with the world watching, she taught us that sometimes discipline is not about pushing through challenges but rather recognizing when to take care of yourself. Biles demonstrated that the strongest move can be choosing your well-being over everything else.

These women are trailblazers who remind me that authenticity, resilience, and self-love are portals to greatness. They inspire me to keep embracing my own path, with all its messiness and magic, and to do it with my head held high. Because at the end of the day, it's not what you achieve but how you live, how you love, and how you stay true to the essence of who you really are.

OWNING YOUR AWESOME

Now that you've got a clearer picture of the qualities you admire, let's make them tangible. Here's an exercise to help you integrate these reflections into your special sauce:

1. **List your top three.** Make a list of three people you admire and jot down the specific qualities that stand out to you. Be as detailed as possible—don't just write "kindness" or "creativity." Describe how these qualities manifest in their lives and what they look like in action.

2. **Reflect on your own life.** You might be surprised to find that these qualities are already a part of your personal approach, quietly influencing your decisions and interactions. If you don't see them yet, consider how you can start embodying these traits more fully.

3. **Set an intention.** Choose one quality from your list and set an intention to cultivate it more consciously in your daily life. This isn't about forcing anything— it's about allowing the quality to flourish naturally as you embrace your true self.

4. **Create a visual reminder.** To keep these reflections front and center, create a vision board, a list on your phone, or even a sticky note on your mirror, reminding you of the qualities you admire.

Let this visual serve as a daily nudge to embody these traits as part of your special sauce.

Remember, this exercise isn't about becoming someone else—it's about recognizing and cultivating the qualities that make you *you*. It's about blending the key ingredients into your special sauce, creating a flavor that's rich, unique, and distinctly yours.

In the end, the qualities you admire in others are like hints from your soul, guiding you toward a fuller expression of your true self. So, embrace them, own them, and let them shine through in everything you do. When you integrate these qualities into your life, you're not just admiring from a distance—you're living them out loud, creating a life that's as flavorful and unique as your special sauce.

WHAT'S YOUR DISTINCT FLAVOR?

Think of your essence as the raw ingredients: your values, your beliefs, the things that drive you, and the qualities you admire in yourself and the world. Now, your distinct flavor is how those ingredients come together and are expressed. It's not just about what's inside—it's about how everything blends together, how it tastes when you present it to others, and how it feels when you're savoring it yourself. Imagine if you were a sauce—what would your flavor be? Bold and spicy, sweet and comforting, or maybe tangy and invigorating? Your flavor isn't about being different just for the sake of difference; it's about being true to who you are. It's about the emotional impact you have on others and, just as importantly, how you feel living in alignment with your true self.

Showcasing your flavor is how you express your essence! It could be through your actions, the way you dress, how you decorate your space, or even the words you choose when you speak. It's undeniably you and applies in any setting. Defining your distinct flavor marks the difference between knowing you're creative and actually infusing that creativity into your everyday life—in the way you solve problems, style yourself, or connect with others.

Your flavor is how your essence manifests in the world. It's what makes your presence memorable long after you've left the room. It's the way you make people feel—whether it's inspired, comforted, or energized. It's like that fun game you play with friends when you ask, "If you were an ice cream flavor, what would you be?" Sure, you might have a favorite flavor, but which one would you actually *be?* (And let me tell you, by unanimous vote, I am always mint chocolate chip. Why? Because mint is refreshing, cool, and leaves a lasting impression. And it's always a nice surprise when you get a little chocolate, because a little sweetness can make all the difference. I am a Cancer/Leo, people!)

CRAFTING YOUR FLAVOR PROFILE

Let's really dig into how your distinct flavor can manifest in your everyday life. Just as different spices and ingredients create a unique dish, your flavor is your essence expressed through the combination of your actions, your interactions, and the energy you bring into the world.

Below are some examples of how flavor shows up (yes, I had fun with this).

THE BOLD SPICER

Imagine someone whose essence is anchored in unwavering strength and a fierce commitment to justice.

This person is the one who always steps up to call out what's wrong, whether it's in the workplace, among friends, or in any situation where fairness is at stake. They're not the type to sit quietly on the sidelines—they stand tall, speak with conviction, and aren't afraid to ruffle feathers when necessary. Their flavor is bold and spicy. They don't just add heat; they change the entire dynamic.

Think about the friend who pushes you to stand up for what you believe in or the coworker who doesn't back down when they know something needs to be addressed. They're the ones who challenge the status quo with confidence, turning passive conversations into action and passive bystanders into allies. The Bold Spicer leaves a lasting impression because they don't just talk about integrity and fairness—they live it out loud, leading by example with every step they take. Their bold flavors redefine the entire dish.

THE COMFORTING SWEETENER

Now, let's look at someone whose essence is compassion and empathy. This person expresses their flavor by being a rock for others, the one you turn to when you need a shoulder to cry on or a kind word to lift your spirits. They're the friend who always knows just what to say to make you feel better, the colleague who goes out of their way to help you out of a jam, or the family member who keeps everyone connected and cared for. Their flavor is sweet and comforting, like a warm cup of tea on a rainy day. They make people feel safe, valued, and understood.

This Comforting Sweetener might show up as the person who organizes care packages for someone going through a tough time or who volunteers at a local shelter, making sure everyone has what they need. Their presence is soothing, and they create spaces characterized by warmth and acceptance. Sweetness isn't just about sugar—it's about adding a touch of comfort that turns any moment into something special.

THE TANGY ENERGIZER

Then, there's the person whose essence is adventure and curiosity. This Tangy Energizer is always on the move, exploring new places, trying new things, and infusing every situation with a burst of excitement. They're the life of the party, the one who persuades everyone to try that new restaurant, or the coworker who suggests the wildest, most creative ideas during brainstorming sessions. Their flavor is tangy and invigorating—they bring a fresh perspective to everything they do and inspire others to step out of their comfort zones.

This might be the friend who's always planning spontaneous weekend trips or the colleague who pushes the team to think outside the box. They're the spark that keeps things lively and interesting, making sure there's never a dull moment. Tangy flavors don't just wake up your taste buds—they wake up your whole world.

THE SAVORY GROUNDER

This person's essence is stability and reliability. They're the one who keeps everything running smoothly, providing a strong foundation for others to build upon. You can count on them in any situation because they're always prepared, always steady, and always there when you need them. Their flavor is savory and grounding, like a hearty stew that warms you from the inside out.

They might manage the behind-the-scenes details to ensure an event goes off without a hitch or be ready with practical advice and a steady hand in a crisis. Their presence is reassuring, and they have a knack for making others feel secure and supported. Savory flavors don't just fill you up—they give you the fuel to keep going.

THE CITRUSY OPTIMIST

This is someone whose essence is positivity and hope. This person has a knack for finding the silver lining in any situation and for spreading joy wherever they go. They're the ones who lift the spirits of everyone around them, whether it's through a kind word, a bright smile, or a contagious laugh. Their flavor is citrusy and refreshing— zesty, bright, and full of life.

They might be the person who sends you a funny meme just when you need a pick-me-up or the one who organizes surprise celebrations to boost team morale at work. They're the one who reminds you that there's always something to smile about, no matter what's going on. Citrusy flavors don't just refresh—they bring a burst of sunshine to your day.

MIX AND MATCH

Personally, I feel like I fall into a "zesty fusion" flavor profile: I've got that bold, direct energy that isn't afraid to call things out, shake things up, and challenge the status quo. But I also try to bring a refreshing, vibrant vibe that energizes and uplifts those around me. As a life coach and a holistic entrepreneur (and a consciousness healer, but that one is sometimes harder to explain on a business card), I aim to infuse my interactions with a soothing, restorative touch, ensuring that even when I'm pushing for change, I'm also nurturing growth and fostering well-being. I'm not just here to stand out—I'm here to inspire, motivate, and leave a lasting, invigorating impact that also brings healing and balance. This flavor aims to be the right blend of strength, positivity, and healing energy that leaves people feeling both empowered and rejuvenated, ready to take on the world with a renewed sense of purpose. (Like I said, I own it.)

Try crafting your personal flavor profile before we tie it all together into your special sauce:

1. **Reflect on your impact.** Think about how you typically make people feel. Do they leave conversations with you feeling inspired, challenged, or comforted? This is a clue to your flavor.

2. **Identify your feelings.** Consider how you want to feel as you go through your life. Do you want to feel energized, peaceful, or engaged? Your flavor is as much about how it makes you feel as it is about others.

3. **Combine your ingredients.** Look at your essence and think about how you can express it in a way that feels right for you. Maybe you're a blend of creativity and calmness, or perhaps you're a mix of determination and warmth.

Sum up your flavor in a statement. For example: *I bring a bold, energizing presence that inspires others to take action,* or *I create a warm, comforting space where people feel valued and heard.* This isn't about being perfect; it's about capturing the essence of how you want to show up in the world.

THE ART OF AUTHENTICITY: UNLEASHING YOUR SPECIAL SAUCE

Alright, we've talked about your essence—the core of who you are—and your distinct flavor, which is how that essence comes to life in the world. But now, we're diving into something deeper: the fearless pursuit of authenticity. This isn't just about knowing who you are or how you show up—it's about living your truth boldly, unapologetically, and with a level of conviction that turns heads and changes the game. Authenticity isn't just a nice concept—it's a way of life. It's about showing up as the real you without filters, masks, or pretense. It's about standing in your truth, even when it's uncomfortable or means going against the grain.

Authenticity makes your special sauce truly special. It takes all those ingredients—your goals, your values, your desires, your essence, your flavor—and turns them into something unforgettable. When you live authentically, you're not just existing—you're making an impact. You're saying to the world, "This is me—take it or leave it," and that's powerful. It's magnetic. The right people, opportunities, and experiences will be drawn to you because you're living in alignment with your true self.

Life Lesson: Authenticity isn't always easy. It requires courage. It demands that you be vulnerable, that you let go of the need for approval, and that you embrace the possibility of rejection or criticism. **Life Frickin' Lesson:** When you live authentically, you give others permission to do the same. You become a beacon for those who are searching for their own truth, which represents the difference between living a life that's good enough and living a life that's deeply fulfilling. It's the unique quality that turns a simple dish into a culinary masterpiece. Without authenticity, your essence and flavor are just ideas. With it, they become action, impact, and legacy.

Your special sauce is the authenticity you slather on the world. We need it. We need you.

CULTIVATING SELF-WORTH AND CONFIDENCE

To live authentically, you need to believe in your worth. This isn't about external validation—it's about knowing, deep down, that you are enough just as you are. Your special sauce is yours and yours alone, and that makes it invaluable.

RECOGNIZING YOUR INHERENT VALUE

Let's get one thing straight: your worth isn't up for debate. It's not some fleeting thing that changes based on who's around or what you've achieved lately. Your value is constant, deeply rooted in the unique essence that only you bring to the table. When you start recognizing this, you stop seeking approval from everyone and their mother. You stop letting other people's opinions dictate how you see yourself. Imagine walking into a room and knowing, deep down, that you don't need anyone else to validate your existence. That's the kind of self-assurance that comes from recognizing your inherent value.

It's like wearing your favorite outfit—not because you want compliments, but because it makes *you* feel good. Think about a time when you accomplished something significant. Maybe you got that promotion, finished a big project, or hit a personal milestone. Now, think about how you felt before anyone else acknowledged it. That feeling of pride, that inner glow? That's your inherent value shining through. Hold on to that, because it's there whether anyone else notices or not.

B uiLDiNG (oNFiDENCE

Confidence isn't about being the loudest voice in the room or the most charismatic person at the party. It's about *knowing* your special sauce and owning it, no matter what. That self-awareness (not your inner critic!) is a gift, an honor, and a privilege to share with others. (*That* is soul-centered living.) It's about standing tall in who you are, even when the world seems intent on shrinking you down.

Confidence is the fuel that keeps you going, even when the way forward isn't clear. It's that inner voice that says, *I've got this,* even when doubt creeps in. It's about embracing who you are, without second-guessing or comparing yourself to others. So, who decided self-doubt was in style? Confidence is your fire—don't let it go out.

Picture this: You're at a meeting or a social event, and the conversation takes a turn toward a topic you're passionate about. Instead of shrinking back, you speak up, sharing your insights with conviction. You're not trying to impress others; you're contributing to the conversation in a way that feels true to you. That's confidence in action. It's not about being the loudest but rather being authentic and trusting that what you bring to the table is valuable. (*Pro tip that we all know deep down:* Insecurity is loud. Confidence isn't necessarily quiet, but it does know how to read the room).

HoNORiNG YOuR STRENGTHS

Your strengths are the homegrown ingredients in your special sauce. They're what make you uniquely you, and when you honor them, you celebrate your talents. This isn't about being boastful or arrogant; it's about recognizing that your gifts are meant to be shared with the world. When you lean into your strengths, you operate in your zone of genius. This is where you shine brightest, where you feel most alive, and where you have the most impact. Honoring your strengths is about giving yourself permission to do more of what you love, to let those natural abilities flow without holding back.

Let's say you've always been great at connecting with people—whether it's networking at events or simply being that friend who everyone turns to for advice. Instead of downplaying this strength, you start to recognize its value. You begin to see how your ability to connect and communicate can open doors in your career, deepen your relationships, and even influence your community. Honoring this strength might mean taking on more leadership roles, mentoring others, or simply being more intentional about how you use your gift.

By celebrating what makes you uniquely you, you embrace your special sauce *and* share it with the world, making your mark in a way that's authentic, impactful, and unmistakably *you*.

EPISODE 16: ARRIVING AT AUTHENTICITY

Authenticity is something I'm often praised for—whether it's in my coaching sessions, my writing, or just the way I move through the world. People often tell me, "That's so you" ("I'm so Julia"—thanks, Charli XCX, for that). I take it as the highest compliment, because it means I'm living in alignment with who I truly am. But here's the thing: this comfort in expressing myself, this confidence in knowing who I am, didn't always come naturally. In fact, it's been a journey—a messy, winding road that's taken me years to navigate.

In my youth, I wasn't always as sure of myself as I am today. I knew who I wanted to be, and I knew the qualities that resonated with me—free-spirited, cool, carefree—but those were also the very things I used as masks. I leaned into those traits because they felt safe, and they were the things that made me feel like I belonged. In doing so, I often stifled the deeper parts of my authenticity, the parts of me that weren't so polished or didn't fit neatly into the boxes I thought I should fit into. As I got older, my understanding of authenticity grew, and it began to surprise me. The things that were truly authentic about me weren't always the qualities I had nurtured or even appreciated. Some were parts of myself I had neglected because they didn't align with the image I was trying to project. There were moments when I realized that my authenticity had been curated, which might sound backward, but it's true. I had been carefully crafting a version of myself that felt safe to share with the world, but it wasn't the whole picture.

Fast-forward to a time when I had established myself as a coach with a thriving business and a solid client base. I finally felt comfortable in my skin, or so I thought. I decided to do something I had always dreamed of: producing my own podcast. I've always been in love with life, with the highs and lows of being human, and I wanted to create a space where I could explore this love openly. My fascination with being human—this wild, unpredictable, magical experience—has been a cornerstone of everything I do. I called the podcast *The Permission Portal*. It was meant to be a literal portal where I gave myself permission to talk about anything and everything related to being human. I imagined it as a space where I could share my love of life, my passion for aliveness, and all the weird, wonderful, and sometimes scary aspects of existing in this world.

But here's where things got tricky: despite my background as an actor, voiceover artist, coach, and public speaker,

I found the podcast format surprisingly challenging. I couldn't quite harness my authenticity in the way I wanted to. I struggled to find my flow, my ease. I started talking about topics I felt I *should* talk about as a coach rather than what truly lit me up and excited me. Even though I enjoyed interviewing experts and loved ones, which allowed me to naturally embody my passion for aliveness, I often found myself wanting to answer the questions I was asking them. Ironically, despite creating a "permission portal," I still couldn't give myself full permission to be *me*. I was praised for my authenticity, my voice, my courage to put myself out there—but inside, I knew I wasn't fully showing up as myself. I eventually slowed down on the podcast, only recording episodes when they aligned with my business or brand. It took me a long time to realize that I hadn't shared my special sauce yet.

My special sauce isn't about being a polished, well-spoken coach. It's about being a little messy, candid, curious, and real. It's about talking openly about how much being alive makes me *feel* alive. It's about helping others by exposing more of myself—not the version that has it all together, but the version that's still figuring it out. And so, as I look to the future, I'm excited about my next podcast idea. This time, I'm determined to give the world a little more of my special sauce. I'll be sharing the space with dear friends who, like me, have unique flavors that the world deserves to experience. Together, we'll dive into the raw, unfiltered aspects of life and talk about what really matters to us. So, keep an eye out for the next one (*Not Another Self-Help Podcast!*),because this time, it's going to be different. This time, it's going to be easy, because I'm finally letting it be.

The point is, even when we think we know ourselves, there's always room to grow into our authenticity. And sometimes that growth comes from the most unexpected sources. For me, it was realizing that I didn't have to fit into the mold of a "respected, educated coach" to make an impact. I just had to be *me*, fully and unapologetically. That's why authenticity is so important—it's the key to unlocking your special sauce, the essence of what makes you truly unique. And once you've got that, everything else falls into place. (*Humble plug:* Consider this the unofficial episode 16 of my podcast. You can hear the other fifteen episodes of *The Permission Portal* on Apple Podcasts or Spotify.)

YOUR SPECIAL SAUCE

Here's the moment we've been building up to: your special sauce. Your special sauce is the culmination of your essence, your flavor, and your authenticity. It's what makes you unforgettable in a world full of sameness. Your special sauce is the alchemy of your life experiences, values, strengths, and that unnameable spark that only you possess. It's what makes your presence felt long after you've left the room. It's the flavor that lingers, the impression that sticks, the energy that inspires.

When you embrace your special sauce, you're not just living—you're creating a legacy. You're showing up in a way that's so unapologetically you that the world has no choice but to take notice. You're not trying to fit in; you're making your own space, your own rules, your own mark. Your special sauce is your signature, your personal brand, the essence of who you are distilled into something tangible and impactful. It's your unique combination of strength, conviction, creativity, and heart. It's what makes you stand out, what makes you a force to be reckoned with. And the best part? It's 100 percent yours. It's the art of being you in a world that often tries to tell you who to be.

CREATING YOUR SPECIAL SAUCE: YOUR UNIQUE RECIPE CARD

With these steps, you're not just creating a recipe—you're crafting a way of life that's uniquely yours. Whether you're jotting down your special sauce on a recipe card or diving deep with the expanded version, remember: this is your secret ingredient. Own it, refine it, and share it with the world. You can add to your personal cookbook and fill in your own recipe card with a downloadable version using the QR code (or give a blank copy to a friend and remind them of their special sauce!).

INGREDIENTS:

→ **2 Cups of Ease:** What you say "yes" to—the things that align with your flow and make life feel effortless

→ **½ Cup of Core Values:** The five key values and nonnegotiables that guide your decisions and actions

→ **½ Cup of Vision:** The clear picture of the life you want to create and how it makes you feel

→ **¼ Cup of Awareness:** A mindful understanding of where you are and what's happening around you

→ **¼ Cup of Acceptance:** Embracing your reality without resistance or judgment

→ **¼ Cup of Aligned Action:** Taking steps that are in sync with your goals and true self

→ **2 Tablespoons of Unique Talents:** The strengths and gifts that make you shine

→ **1 Tablespoon of Deep Desire:** The powerful desire statement that keeps you focused and motivated on your journey

→ **3 Teaspoons of Triple Threat:** A balanced blend of mind, body, and spirit

→ **1 Heaping Teaspoon of Passion:** What fuels you and ignites your inner fire

→ **A Dash of Authenticity:** Your true self, unfiltered and genuine

→ **A Pinch of Vulnerability:** The courage to be open and real, even when it's uncomfortable

→ **A Sprinkle of Boldness:** The confidence to stand out, take risks, and make your mark

INSTRUCTIONS:

1. **Prep your dish with purpose.** Before adding anything else, coat your base with a clear sense of intention. This sets the stage for everything to come, ensuring that every ingredient you add aligns with your true self and ultimate vision.

2. **Start with ease.** Begin by recognizing what aligns with your flow—the things that make life feel effortless. These are your "yes" moments, the foundation that sets the tone for your special sauce.

3. **Add your deep desire.** Stir in that powerful desire

statement that keeps you motivated. This is the heartbeat of your sauce, giving it purpose and direction.

4. **Incorporate awareness.** Mix in a quarter cup of awareness—be mindful of where you are and what's happening around you. This will ground your sauce, ensuring it's well balanced and in touch with reality.

5. **Blend in acceptance.** Pour in acceptance, embracing your reality without resistance. This ingredient allows your sauce to develop depth and complexity, making it richer and more satisfying.

6. **Stir in aligned action.** Next, add aligned action— take steps that are in sync with your goals and true self. This is what brings everything together, ensuring that your sauce isn't just flavorful but also purposeful.

7. **Mix in your core values.** Fold in your core values—the nonnegotiable principles that guide your life. These are the essential ingredients that shape the character of your sauce.

8. **Incorporate vision.** Add a half cup of vision—the clear picture of the life you want to create. This ingredient gives your sauce direction and depth, adding layers of flavor that reflect your aspirations.

9. **Blend the triple threat.** Sprinkle in a balanced blend of mind, body, and spirit. This trio ensures your sauce is holistic, nourishing every part of your being.

10. **Mix in unique talents.** Now, add your unique

strengths and gifts. These are the distinct flavors that make your sauce stand out and leave a memorable taste.

11. **Stir in authenticity.** Pour in a dash of your true self—unfiltered and genuine. This is where your sauce really starts to come alive, full of personality and character.

12. **Add vulnerability.** Don't shy away from adding a pinch of vulnerability. It may seem risky, but it's the ingredient that deepens the flavor, adding a richness that's both authentic and irresistible.

13. **Spice with passion.** Stir in a heaping teaspoon of passion—the fire that fuels you. This is the kick that gives your sauce its signature zing, making it unforgettable.

14. **Finish with boldness.** Finally, top it off with a sprinkle of boldness. This is the confidence that elevates your sauce from good to extraordinary, ensuring it leaves a lasting impression.

15. **Let it simmer.** Allow your sauce to simmer and blend. Take the time to taste, adjust, and perfect it as you grow and evolve. Don't rush this step—good things take time.

16. **Serve it up.** Now, it's time to share your special sauce with the world. Whether it's in your work, your relationships, or just how you show up every day, let your unique flavor shine through. This is your creation—own it, enjoy it, and watch how it leaves others wanting more.

SHARE YOUR SAUCE

So, as we move forward, remember this: the world needs your flavor, your unique blend of strength, passion, and authenticity. Embrace it, refine it, and serve it with pride. When you live authentically, you're not just adding to the conversation—you're transforming it.

Mantra: *I am the creator of my own flavor, the master of my own recipe. My special sauce is what sets me apart, what makes me unforgettable, and what drives me to live authentically, boldly, and without apology.*

You've mixed your special sauce and perfected your flavor—nice work, chef! But before you start dishing it out to the world, let's talk about what happens when the kitchen heats up. Life's going to throw you curveballs, and that's where perspective comes in. It's time to widen that window of tolerance so that you can handle whatever comes your way, with grace, grit, and a sprinkle of your signature spice. Ready to see the world with fresh eyes and an expanded palate? Let's open the kitchen window and let the world smell what's cooking.

CHAPTER 9

EXPANDING THE WINDOW OF TOLERANCE

*"Re-examine all you have been told.
Dismiss what insults your soul."*

—Walt Whitman

PERSPECTIVE IS EVERYTHING

"Expanding the window of tolerance" is a concept borrowed from psychology, referring to the range of emotional experiences we can comfortably handle. It means increasing the capacity to handle life's ups and downs without getting thrown off course, as well as being open to redefining what success and fulfillment look like for you, even when it feels uncomfortable.

This chapter is about widening your capacity to embrace new perspectives, navigate uncharted territory, and handle life's inevitable surprises with grace (when you and I are done here, that is, and the world around you comes callin' again). I want to share ways to expand your ability to keep moving forward, even when the road gets a little bumpy, and to let your authentic self shine, no matter the circumstances. But there's more to it. This chapter isn't just about tolerating more; it's about embracing the ripple effect of the transformation you've already set in motion. You've committed to a life that gets to be easy—let that sink in for a moment. You've done the work to uncover your special sauce, and now it's time to see how those changes affect the world around you.

This is where you take that deeply personal understanding of who you are and apply it to the wider world, challenging old definitions and embracing a broader, more open-minded approach to life. By expanding your window of tolerance, you put the theory of authenticity into practice, as a way of life that can adapt, grow, and thrive in any situation. This chapter will help you prepare to step into the world with a resilience and openness that reflect your true self. You've got the tools, the mindset, and the clarity compass all dialed in. This is where we slow down, take stock, and make sure everything is in alignment before we hit the ground running with our new, easier life.

Think of this chapter as that moment in the kitchen right before you take the lid off a simmering pot of something delicious. You've been adding ingredients, tasting, and adjusting, and now you're standing there with a spoon in hand, ready for the big reveal. Not only are you chef, you're also the recipe creator, the critic, and the lucky diner who gets to savor every bite.

Success, fulfillment, ease—they aren't rigid blueprints to follow. This process is more like a living, breathing thing—constantly shifting, growing, and taking on new forms. It's about embracing the twists and turns, allowing those unexpected moments to shape us in ways we never imagined, and having the guts to live in alignment with what really matters to us. Before we dive headfirst into expanding our window of tolerance and embracing the challenges that shape our true selves, let's hit pause. It's time to take a quick inventory and make sure all the rewiring we've done is in perfect alignment. Don't rush to the finish line just yet (the process is everything). Let's ensure you're ready to move forward with intention and clarity.

That's exactly why I dropped a little Walt Whitman here. He's the perfect literary companion for this chapter. As his quote says above, "Re-examine all you have been told. Dismiss what insults your soul." It's basically a poetic permission slip to question everything you've been fed about success and fulfillment (and I figured we'd lean into the literary mind of a nineteenth-century poet after our Disney deep dives).

Whitman was a key figure in the Transcendentalist movement, which emphasized the importance of individualism, self-reliance, and the inherent goodness of people and nature. This particular quote embodies Whitman's philosophy of questioning societal norms, traditions, and beliefs that do not resonate with one's inner self. It's a call to introspection and critical thinking, urging individuals to reassess the values and information that have been imposed on them by society, culture, or authority figures. If something feels wrong or conflicts with one's own sense of truth or morality, Whitman advises rejecting it in favor of what aligns with the soul's deeper understanding. (Ditto.)

Whitman was all about embracing the messy, raw, and real parts of life, and that's precisely what expanding your window of tolerance entails. So, take his words to heart: question the status quo, toss out what doesn't align with your soul, and push yourself to open that window wider—

there's a whole world waiting on the other side. (Somehow, my window always opens to the jungle.)

SURVIVING AND THRIVING IN THE JUNGLE (AGAIN)

Not too long ago, I found myself at the Envision Festival in Costa Rica, in a situation that was a bit outside my usual festival-going routine. An idea had been on my mind for over a year, simmering quietly until it finally boiled over into action. Instead of showing up as a guest, glittered and ready to dance, I felt this instinct—this wild, undeniable pull—to attend the festival as part of the team, to serve rather than just soak it all in. So, with a mix of determination and a dash of persistence, I snagged one of the last spots on the yoga facilitation team. And no, I'm not a yogi, but I figured if I could find a way to be a part of the crew, to really immerse myself in the experience beyond just partying, I was going to do it.

I didn't have any clear expectations, and I honestly wasn't sure what I was looking to get out of my role. But there I was, pitching my little tent next to a marsh full of bugs that could double as small aircraft and battling suffocating heat, a stomach that turned on me more than once, and shifts that started before sunrise or stretched until midnight. And you know what? I found that I actually loved it—the whole gritty, sweaty, exhausting mess of it. There was something magical about the community, the shared generosity, and yes, even the cinnamon rolls that became my lifeline after the majority of us fell victim to the inevitable jungle stomach rot. (No shame there—it felt like a rite of passage, one I embraced humbly as I found myself face down on the jungle floor, medics circling before I stubbornly rose hours later to finish my shift and make it to the ecstatic dance floor that night. And, for the record, I was stone-cold sober the entire time.)

I met some of the best people I've ever known—kindhearted, generous souls who were just as worn out and just as determined to make it through each day as I was. Sure, we had food and water, so it wasn't exactly Survivor, but in many ways, for us, it was survival. And somehow, I didn't just survive—I thrived. I found myself not wanting to return to the so-called "real world." I wanted to wake up to music, greet every person with a smile, dance every night, and laugh with these incredible people I'd grown to love, each in their own way. My friends back home couldn't help but laugh when I told them I'd be living in a tent in the jungle for a week, working instead of attending, at the bottom of the totem pole instead of running the show. But I loved every minute of it. I expanded my window of tolerance by discovering my strength, tenacity, and vitality and by realizing just how adaptable I could be. I didn't need much, and that simplicity brought me immense joy.

My entire perspective on success shifted in that jungle, and not just in the small, everyday ways we often talk about. I'm talking about a deep, foundational shift—the kind that changes how you see everything. Before this experience, success had always been tied to achievements, milestones, and how well I could check off the boxes that society had set for me or I had set for myself. But something happened out there, amid the heat, the bugs, and the unexpected friendships. Success took on a new shape. It wasn't about external accolades or how impressive my life looked from the outside. Success, for me, became about the simple yet profound moments: Did I laugh? Did I smile? Did I witness something beautiful? Did I lighten someone's day, nourish my body, hydrate myself, move, dance, and serve others with a full heart?

In that jungle, stripped of the comforts and distractions of modern life, I realized that these small, seemingly insignificant acts were where true success lived. They were the moments that brought joy, connection, and a sense of purpose. My special sauce—my authentic self—flourished in this environment, and I saw firsthand how powerful it could be when I let it shine without the usual filters or expectations. People responded to and connected with that authenticity, and it became clear to me that this was the version of myself I needed to bring into the rest of my life. This realization gave me the permission I didn't even know I was seeking—to bring these fresh perspectives home with me and to let them reshape the way I live, work, and interact with the world. It wasn't just about having an enlightening experience in the jungle and then returning to business as usual. It was about questioning everything I thought I knew about success, fulfillment, and what really matters. It was about revising my life to support these new, more authentic definitions.

After returning from the jungle, it felt like I'd set a ripple effect in motion, touching every aspect of my life. The insights I gained in that wild, untamed environment didn't stay there—they followed me home, subtly reshaping my world. It was like a spell had been cast, enchanting everything around me. My interactions became more authentic, my work more meaningful—and people began to respond differently to me, as if they too were touched by the same magic. Not everything was smooth; some relationships struggled to adapt, resisting the new energy I brought into the world. However, as I leaned into this transformation, new connections flourished, drawn to the real, unfiltered me. This ripple of change wasn't just a gentle wave—it was a powerful current guiding me toward a life that felt more aligned, vibrant, and true to who I am. And the most beautiful part? It didn't stop with me. My transformation inspired others, creating a chain reaction of authenticity and growth that reached far beyond what I could have imagined.

This chapter is about understanding and embracing the ripple effect of transformation. When you change, everything around you changes too. Some things will naturally fall away, making space for new growth, while others will rise up to meet the new energy you bring. It's all part of the process, and the more you lean into it, the more you'll see that this ripple effect isn't something to fear—it's the very essence of how true, lasting change happens. I asked myself what was possible just by showing up, and I endeavored to make my life even easier.

With these principles in mind, let's start by asking ourselves the real questions—the ones that dig beneath the surface and push us to reconsider what we're truly striving for. What questions are you asking yourself now, and are they leading you to the life you want to live?

WHAT ARE YOU REALLY ASKING?

Alright, let's cut to the chase. The way you talk to yourself? Those inner monologues and random thoughts? They're not just background noise—they're basically the script for your entire life. Ever notice how the questions you ask yourself can totally shift your mood, your decisions, and even your whole day? Have you noticed I've been doing that in every chapter? Do you notice I'm doing it now? That's because the questions you ask are the ones setting the stage for how you show up in the world.

Life Lesson: If those questions are on autopilot, programmed by what you think you *should* want or what everyone else is doing, then you're probably playing a role you didn't even audition for. The questions you ask aren't just mental fluff—they're the plot twists that drive your story forward. So, let's get intentional about what we're asking, because that's where we make shifts happen. I'm not talking about just tweaking your mindset—I'm talking about rewriting the whole damn screenplay and making sure you're the star of a life that's actually yours.

When I work with clients as a coach, the pathway to purpose often starts with the questions we choose to explore. Just like in therapy, the way a question is framed can determine the quality of the answer we arrive at. Ask a limiting question, and you'll get a limiting answer. But ask a question that opens doors (or the window of tolerance in this case) by challenging old beliefs, and you'll find new pathways you never knew existed.

Now that you have calibrated your clarity compass, invested in yourself, and gotten acquainted with your values, vision, and that mind-body-spirit trifecta, it's time to put those tools to work. You're not a beginner anymore—you're equipped with some serious life-navigation skills. So, let's dive into some self-inquiry. Think about the questions you're asking yourself every day. Are they propelling you forward, or are they keeping you stuck in the same old patterns? Are they coming from a place of genuine desire, or are they just echoes of what you think you *should* want? You've already done the work to understand what matters to you, so now it's about aligning those questions with your true north.

For example, instead of asking, "What will make me successful?"—which (loving call out!) usually means chasing someone else's idea of success—try asking, "What will make me truly happy?" Go beyond superficial happiness to what brings you deep, lasting fulfillment. The first question might have you running after external validation—impressive on the outside, sure, but hollow on the inside. By contrast, the second question taps into what really lights you up and fills your life with peace, joy, and satisfaction. You're in control now, equipped with all the tools you've gathered. The questions you ask should focus on shaping a life that fits you perfectly, not one molded by someone else's expectations. This is about living in alignment with your true self, using everything you've learned to guide you toward what truly matters.

Here's another example: instead of asking, "Why does this always happen to me?" try reframing it as "What can I learn from this situation?" The first question assumes you're a victim of circumstance, stuck in a cycle of bad luck or failure. The second question empowers you. It shifts the focus from what's happening to you to what you can take from the experience and how you can grow.

In relationships, the questions you ask can either build bridges or walls. Consider the difference between asking your partner, "Why don't you ever listen to me?" versus "How can we communicate better so we both feel heard?" The first question is accusatory and defensive, likely to trigger a negative response. The second one invites collaboration, understanding, and a shared effort to improve the relationship. It's about shifting from blame to solution, from conflict to connection.

The questions you ask yourself are about to become your next big tool in letting life be easy. Think of it this way: now that you've done the work of getting to know yourself better, you can use that self-awareness to start reframing the way you approach everything in your life. The right questions can help you break down old, limiting beliefs and expand your window of tolerance, which is another way of saying that you're going to challenge the way you think, stretch your capacity to handle life, and open yourself up to new possibilities.

SUBCONSCIOUS SPRING CLEANING

It's time for a little subconscious spring cleaning. Think of it like clearing out the lower shelves of your pantry after you've nailed the big recipe. You've done the deep work, but before you can fully expand and step into what's next, there's still some clutter hanging around in the corners. Those old mental habits, lingering doubts, and outdated beliefs? They need to go. This isn't about starting over—it's about clearing the way for what's ahead.

With all you know now, this purge is essential to keeping the path clear as you move forward and respond to the shifts that are bound to come. You're going through what no longer feels good and doesn't serve your authentic self anymore, and you're redefining what you want to hold on to as you move forward. This is where you get to apply your special sauce in a way that's more aligned with who you are now, using the clarity and wisdom you've gained to shape a life that feels right, feels easy, and, most importantly, feels like you.

VAMPiNG UP VALUES

You've already done the heavy lifting of digging deep and identifying your core values. You've peeled back the layers and figured out what really matters to you, what drives you, and what you're all about. But here's the thing: life isn't static, and neither are you. So, why are we doing this exercise now? As you've grown, learned, and evolved over the course of these pages (come on, give yourself that credit!), your values might have shifted. Maybe just a little, maybe a lot. So let's reassess and see where you stand.

Think of it as a values checkup—because what was true for you yesterday might not be true today, and that's perfectly okay. This process is like going through your closet for that tediously necessary (yet ultimately satisfying) seasonal cleaning. Remember that favorite jacket you used to wear everywhere? The one that made you feel unstoppable? Well, maybe it doesn't quite fit the same way anymore. Maybe your style has evolved and now your vibe needs a refresher. The same goes for your values. We're here to make sure that what's hanging in your mental wardrobe still fits and feels good to wear.

Here's the plan: Grab a moment of quiet and a cup of something soul-soothing. (A glass of wine or a ginger shot? You know best now!) Revisit those core values you identified earlier. Ask yourself, *Do they still resonate? Do they still reflect who I am today?* Maybe ambition and discipline were your driving forces. You were all about climbing the ladder, making a name for yourself, and pushing through long hours because that's what you believed success looked like. You valued the grind because it seemed like the only way to get ahead, and you took pride in your relentless work ethic. But now, after dedicating time to nurturing your mind, body, and spirit, you've realized that constant hustle isn't sustainable. You've seen the toll it can take on your well-being—maybe it's burnout, stress, or just the sheer exhaustion of always being "on." Balance and well-being have started to nudge their way to the top of your list. Now, success doesn't just mean achieving the next milestone; it also means having the time and energy to enjoy your life, to breathe, and to be present.

Maybe you've always valued security—whether it's financial security, job stability, or a predictable routine. Security provided a sense of comfort and control, especially in uncertain times. But now, after exploring your passions and diving into personal growth, you find that you're craving adventure and spontaneity. You're drawn to the idea of taking risks and stepping into the unknown, because you've realized that's where true growth happens. Adventure and spontaneity might start to edge out security as your top values as you begin to prioritize experiences that challenge you and push you out of your comfort zone. Or perhaps compassion was always something you valued in theory—you cared about others, but your focus was on personal achievement. However, as you've grown, you've experienced the power of empathy and kindness—in how you treat both others and yourself. Compassion has now become a cornerstone of your values, guiding your interactions and decisions in ways that uplift both you and those around you.

GOAL DETOX

Once you've got your updated values in place, it's time to line them up with your current goals. Do your goals and values align, or have you been chasing after things that no longer serve the person you've become? If there's a mismatch, it's time for a little goal detox. This might mean letting go of ambitions that aren't really yours anymore and embracing new ones that align with your special sauce. To do a quick goal detox, start by listing your current goals and comparing them with your newly updated values. Ask yourself if each goal aligns with who you are now. If a goal feels outdated or no longer resonates, it's time to let it go. Focus on creating new goals that genuinely reflect your current values and aspirations, ensuring they guide you toward a life that feels more authentic and fulfilling. Trust your clarity compass to navigate this process with ease.

Your goals direct your energy, time, and resources. If they're not aligned with your current values and vision, you're likely to end up somewhere that doesn't feel right or fulfilling. When your goals are misaligned with who you truly are, you're constantly operating outside of your window of tolerance—straining to achieve things that don't resonate with your core values. This misalignment can lead to stress, burnout, and a feeling of being off course. On the other hand, when your goals align with your reassessed values, you're better equipped to handle the ups and downs of the journey, because you're working toward something that genuinely matters to you. This alignment broadens your ability to stay grounded and resilient in the face of challenges, allowing you to operate within an expanded window of tolerance and making growth, fulfillment, and ease more attainable.

The goal detox is about refining your path with the wisdom you've gained. It's about being proactive in shaping a life that feels good, that makes sense for who you are now, and that's grounded in the clarity and understanding you've cultivated. We could spend a whole chapter on goals, but you've got this! Goals are truly measured by how they resonate with your own sense of success, so trust yourself to craft goals that your clarity compass can navigate with ease.

CLEARING OUT THE CLUTTER

Now that you've tidied up your internal world, it's time to shift your focus to the external. Expanding your window of tolerance means letting go of the things you once thought were essential but no longer serve you and prioritizing what genuinely makes your life easier. Your environment isn't just the backdrop to your life—it's the stage, the props, and sometimes even the director calling the shots. If your surroundings aren't vibing with your current self, it's time to clear the stage and set up something that's truly in alignment. This is about creating an entire atmosphere that exudes ease.

Start with the obvious: your physical space. Look around—does your environment inspire you, or does it make you feel like you're drowning in stuff? It's time to channel your inner Virgo (they are more efficient in this area) and ask yourself if each item you own is serving a purpose. And don't just think about what you see. Open those drawers, dive into that closet, and clear out the nooks and crannies. Less is more, darling. (*Pro tip:* If it's covered with dust or hasn't seen the light of day in months, it's probably time to say goodbye.)

Clearing out the old isn't just about making room—it's about creating an environment that actively supports the new, more aligned you. Whether that means refreshing your decor, shifting your daily routines, or surrounding yourself with people who inspire and uplift you, the goal is to build a space—both physically and emotionally—that feels like a sanctuary for your growth.

By physically and emotionally clearing out what no longer serves you, you do more than make space—you create an environment where you can thrive. Your mind, your heart, your space, your life: this is your stage, your kitchen, and your sanctuary, and it deserves to be filled with nothing but the best. And don't worry, we're not letting relationships off the hook either—this is just the appetizer before we dig into the main course.

REDEFINING RELATIONSHIPS

As your goals and values level up, it's time to turn your attention to the people you surround yourself with. This is the moment when you acknowledge that the people in your life—the ones you say yes to, the ones you admire, and even the ones who might drain your energy—play a significant role in shaping your journey. Think of your relationships as the enchanted forest in which your new self is embarking on a grand adventure. Some of these connections are like the magical trees and mystical creatures that guide and protect you, offering wisdom and strength as you journey forward. Others, however, might be more like hidden traps or lurking shadows, quietly sapping your energy and hindering your progress.

As the hero of your own story, it's essential to ensure that the path you walk is filled with allies and supportive forces, not obstacles that drain your vitality or block your way. This is the ripple effect of transformation, and it's both powerful and, sometimes, a bit unsettling. (Let's be honest, though: everyone's a little bit of an antihero, so approach this process with love.)

THE ENERGY VAMPiRES

Let's hold up a mirror to the energy vampires (since they often can't see themselves clearly). Picture them as the shadowy figures lurking in the corners of your enchanted forest—the ones who drain your energy and cast a gloom over your path. You know who they are—the people who leave you feeling drained, stressed, or out of alignment with your values. Maybe it's the friend who always seems to be in the middle of a crisis but never asks how you're doing, or the colleague who brings more drama than productivity to your workday.

These energy vampires may have found their way into your life before you began your journey of transformation, but now, as you expand your window of tolerance and grow into your new self, you'll find they don't quite belong in your forest anymore. Just as you'd clear out stale air by opening a window, it's crucial to clear out stale energy in your relationships. This doesn't necessarily mean cutting people off entirely; sometimes it's about setting healthier boundaries or reevaluating how much time and energy you're willing to invest.

It's time to wield your metaphorical stake and perform an energy cleanse.

1. **Identify the vampires.** Start by taking a clear-eyed look at your relationships. Who leaves you feeling depleted after every interaction? Who consistently brings negativity into your life? (Cue the dramatic organ music.) Jot down a list of people who fit this description—those who sap your energy without giving anything positive in return. (You're goin' on a vampire hunt, honey!)

2. **Assess the impact.** Next, evaluate how these relationships impact you. Are they preventing you from growing or moving forward? Do they clash with your core values? Understanding the specific ways these energy vampires affect you will help clarify why it's essential to make a change. (Remember, even garlic bread can't save a relationship that's gone stale.)

3. **Set clear boundaries.** Once you've identified the energy vampires, it's time to set boundaries. This doesn't have to be a dramatic confrontation. Start by limiting your exposure. Maybe you don't answer every call or text immediately, or you cut down the time you spend with them—but also, don't be afraid to be transparent about what you are focusing on. This isn't about ghosting (because vampires have different powers, duh); it's about respectfully affirming what you'll say yes or no to. Be firm but kind. Let them know what you can and cannot

tolerate moving forward. (Rather than poisoning apples, you're growing them.)

4. **Communicate with compassion.** If it's a relationship you value and want to salvage, have an honest conversation. Explain how certain behaviors or patterns affect you and what you need to feel more balanced and respected. Use "I" statements to avoid sounding accusatory. For example, you might say, "I feel drained when our conversations focus on negativity. I'd like to focus on more uplifting topics." This isn't about pulling out the receipts or the blame game; it's about expressing what feels true for you and accepting that this is actually an act of love. (Sometimes the most loving thing is the hardest: old **Life Lesson**, but true.)

5. **Reevaluate the relationship.** After setting boundaries, observe how the energy vampire responds. Do they respect your limits, or do they push against them? Are they willing to meet you halfway, or do they continue draining your energy? Based on their response, decide whether this relationship can continue in a healthier way or if it's time to distance yourself further. (Are they hissing at the sunlight you've let in?)

6. **Make space for growth.** As you clear out the energy vampires, you'll notice an opening in your life. Fill that space with relationships that nurture and inspire you—those who are like the sunlight and water in your enchanted forest. Seek out connections that align with your values and support your growth. (I like to believe that everyone is a unicorn in their own special way. So rather than saying surround yourself with unicorns, let's be bold and lean into surrounding yourself with

dragons, not trolls. And yes, in my fantasy world, dragons are the good guys.)

7. **Regular energy checks.** Finally, make this a regular practice. Just as you wouldn't let weeds overrun your garden, keep an eye on the energy dynamics in your relationships. (Weeds? Or maybe bats—let's stay on theme here.) Periodically assess whether your relationships are still serving you, and be proactive about making adjustments as needed. (Because, darling, you're the one with the enchanted forest. Keep it thriving. We've been in kitchens, boats, roads, and forests. The modern world gets to be a piece of cake.)

EXPANDING YOUR ECOSYSTEM

Let's talk about those relationships that don't just pass the vibe check—they elevate it. These are the people who align with your newly defined values and goals, the ones who get you on a soul-deep level. They're the ones who see your potential, who get excited when you start sharing your latest epiphanies, and who are right there with you, cheering you on (or, even better, joining you on the journey).

These are your kindred spirits, your support system, your ecosystem. In the enchanted forest of your life, they're the wise sages, the free-spirited centaurs, and the fellow adventurers who walk the path with you. They don't just tolerate your growth—they celebrate it with the joy of a shared victory. They're not intimidated by your evolution; instead, they're inspired by it, seeing it as a sign that the whole forest is flourishing. They're the sunlight that warms your leaves, the water that nourishes your roots, and the rich soil that supports your every step.

These are the companions who make your enchanted forest thrive, nurturing your growth and keeping you grounded in your truth, even when the winds of change blow through. Together, you're crafting a magical space where everyone's unique qualities add to the beauty and strength of the whole.

So, how do you nurture these golden connections? Start by reaching out—express your appreciation, and let them know how much they mean to you. Deepen these bonds by spending time together, sharing your dreams, and supporting each other's growth by showing up or practicing conscious (direct and compassionate) communication. These relationships will fuel your journey, helping you stay true to your path even when the road gets rocky. Remember, these connections are your lifeline. They're the ones who will remind you of who you are when you start to doubt yourself and who will stand by you when the rest of the world seems to misunderstand your vision. So, invest in these relationships, pour into them as much as they pour into you, and watch how they help you flourish in ways you never imagined. They will help you stay aligned with your true north, guiding you forward with love, support, and a shared commitment to living authentically.

As you navigate these shifts, it's more important than ever to build a support system that truly aligns with your values and goals. This might mean seeking out new communities, new mentors, or even reconnecting with people who share your vision. Surround yourself with those who will help you sustain the changes you're making, who will hold you accountable, and who will celebrate your growth. As you do so, keep your focus on your values, alignment, growth, and authenticity. The relationships that remain, the ones you nurture, and the new ones you build will all contribute to the life of ease and fulfillment you've committed to.

Life Lesson: Just like a well-tended ecosystem, your relationships need care, attention, and sometimes a bit of pruning. As you expand your window of tolerance and step into this next phase, trust that the right people will be there to support you—and that you'll have the wisdom to know who those people are.

Here's a reality check: not all relationships will survive the changes you're making, and that's okay. Change has a ripple effect—it starts with you, but it inevitably touches those around you. As you grow, some people might not understand the new you. They might question your choices or even pull away because your growth makes them uncomfortable. This can be hard to accept, but it's also a necessary part of the process.

When you encounter this dynamic, it's essential to communicate your changes with compassion and clarity. Explain your new mindset, your goals, and why these changes are important to you. Be prepared for resistance or skepticism—change is hard for everyone, not just for you. But stay true to your path, and remember that those who are meant to be in your life will adapt, grow with you, or at least respect your journey.

THE RIPPLE EFFECT OF TRANSFORMATION

As you've journeyed through this book, you've learned to clear out the clutter—whether it's mental, physical, or relational—and make space for a life that's easier, more aligned, and authentically yours. But here's the thing: change, real change, isn't just about the big, bold moves. It's also about what happens after. It's about embracing the ripple effects, navigating the unknown, and learning to stay grounded when the ground itself feels like it's shifting beneath your feet.

Let's get real: change isn't always comfortable. In fact, it can be downright unsettling. But here's the **Life Lesson** no one really teaches us: discomfort is often where the magic happens. I've been saying it in every chapter (using every analogy possible, and if you've been keeping up, I am utterly impressed!). By asking for ease, you asked for change. You identified that something about you or the life you're living is out of alignment with your most authentic self, and you decided to change it. No matter what tools, insights, or perspectives I share, real change and transformation challenge every part of you, making you confront whether those changes are truly worth the effort.

You're going to be tested, shaken, and thrown off balance until the chaos becomes a dance. The moment you start dancing with these changes instead of resisting them, life begins to ease up. This is where real growth happens—where you push past your old limits and start seeing both the world and yourself in a whole new light. Change is inevitable, and if it is intentional—just like your relationships, your environments, your habits, and everything else we covered—your feelings about being alive will transform into something better than you ever could've imagined. Growth can be brutal, but it's also a process of expansion and enhancement.

Change is the only constant in life—yes, it's a cliché, but it's also a universal truth. Whether it's a career shift, a relationship evolving, or an unexpected twist in your life's plot, change will happen. The sooner you accept that fact, the easier it will be to navigate the shifting tides. Think of change like the seasons—each one brings its own challenges and beauty, and each one prepares you for the next. The key is to remain flexible and open-minded, like a tree that bends in the wind but doesn't break.

So, how do you do that? Start by building resilience. Just as you've cleared out the physical and emotional clutter, now it's time to fortify your inner landscape. Resilience isn't about being tough or stoic; it's about being adaptable, about having the inner strength to bounce back from whatever life throws at you. Cultivate practices that strengthen your emotional and mental resilience—whether it's mindfulness, meditation, journaling, or simply giving yourself permission to rest when you need it. Be patient with yourself, and remember that self-compassion is your best ally during times of change. You have a pantry full of tools and resources to choose from in the quest for ease.

As you expand your window of tolerance and step into the unknown, it's natural to feel a mix of emotions—excitement, anxiety, joy, and maybe even grief for the life you're leaving behind. This emotional landscape is part of the journey. Allow yourself to feel it all, and remember to treat yourself with the same kindness and compassion you'd offer a close friend.

The unknown can be a scary place—after all, it's full of uncertainty, and humans are wired to crave stability. But here's a little secret: the unknown is also where the potential for growth lies. It's the blank page where you get to write the next chapter of your life. Rather than fearing the unknown, learn to embrace it as a space for possibility.

To prepare for the unknown, first, build a supportive network—surround yourself with people who get your journey and can offer strength when you need it. Have strategies ready for tough times, like a mantra, breathing exercise, or playlist that centers you. Understand that not everyone will align with your growth—that's okay. Use clear, compassionate communication, focusing on how you feel and what you need. Manage emotions with patience, but stay firm in your boundaries. This is your life, and you deserve to live it authentically. Finally, recognize that as you embrace change in your life, you become a conduit for change in the lives of others. Your transformation has a ripple effect—it inspires those around you to look at their own lives, to question their own status quo, and maybe, just maybe, to start their own journey toward ease and authenticity. And that, my friend, is a beautiful thing. Change is not something to be feared; it's something to be embraced, celebrated, and welcomed as a constant companion on your journey.

As we close this chapter, take a deep breath. You've done the work, and you're ready for whatever comes next. The unknown isn't a void; it's a canvas. And you, with all the wisdom you've gathered, are more than capable of painting a life that's vibrant, fulfilling, and truly your own. So go ahead—step into the change, and watch the ripples of your transformation spread far and wide.

Think of how much cooking we've done in this book. Imagine the aromas, the energy, and the love that is radiating from your proverbial kitchen. You've been crafting the recipe and doing what you can to get it just right. This is the moment you crack open the window and let that scrumptious creation fill the air.

So, before we put the finishing touches on your ease blueprint, I leave you with one final step. More importantly, I leave you with one last choice.

THE PLEDGE OF ALLEGIANCE TO YOURSELF

I want to guide you through one last powerful exercise. It's not just a tool or a resource; it's a pledge—a deep, unshakeable commitment to yourself. This isn't about making a promise to be perfect or to have it all figured out.

It's about standing tall in who you are, embracing every facet of your being, and vowing to show up fully in your life, no matter what challenges come your way. This is an oath.

In one of my more recent ayahuasca ceremonies, I asked my guides, my angels, and my intuition for something to anchor me when life feels overwhelming. Guided by the wisdom of ayahuasca (which feels like another familiar voice in my head, in addition to my own thoughts and intuition), I was brought to a moment of deep clarity. In that sacred space, I was asked to sit up, to look within, and to pledge allegiance to my true self. It was a pledge to remain unwavering in my authenticity, to honor my journey, and to trust that even when life shakes me to my core, that core— my true self—would remain unshakeable.

I want to acknowledge that sharing insights from my experiences, like ayahuasca, can resonate differently with each person. I'm not suggesting, advising, or influencing anyone to take this path. What I'm offering is the wisdom I gained from my journey—something meaningful that I've applied in my own life. I drank the tea, so you don't have to (literally and several times).

At that moment, I realized the profound importance of this commitment. It wasn't just about the act of pledging; it was about the deep connection to who I am at my essence. It was a reminder that no matter how turbulent life may become, no matter how many challenges arise, I could always return to this pledge as my foundation. It's about standing firm in my truth, embracing every part of my journey, and knowing that this pledge is a commitment to live authentically, with courage and grace.

This pledge became a beacon I could return to whenever doubt or confusion crept in. I made the choice to be me, no matter how hard it was. This is the choice I want to share with you, dear reader: a pledge of allegiance to your true self, a promise to honor who you are, and to stand firm in your authenticity, no matter what life brings your way.

This is your moment. This is your pledge. You've done the work, expanded your window of tolerance, and embraced the ripple effects of transformation. Now, it's time to seal the deal. Make a promise to yourself that transcends any challenge, any doubt, or any fear—a promise to be, in the truest sense, you.

I pledge allegiance to myself,
To the essence of who I am,
To the truths I've uncovered,
To the light and the shadow within.

I vow to honor my journey,
To walk my path with courage and grace,
To embrace the changes that come,
Knowing they are part of my growth.

I commit to living authentically,
To showing up fully and unapologetically,
To loving myself in all my forms,
And to trusting that I am enough.

I choose now, in this moment, to feel all my feelings
And to create space for those and
that which light up my soul.
I pledge to let go of those and that
which make me question myself
Or in any way make me feel unlovable.

I pledge allegiance to ease,
To a life that gets to be easy,
Because I am worthy and I am

capable of being the person
And of living the life I deeply desire.

No matter what life throws my way,
I will remain steadfast in my truth,
Rooted in the core of who I am,
Unshakeable, unbreakable, and whole.
This is my power, my promise,
And I pledge allegiance to myself
For now and forever.

Carry this pledge with you as you move forward. You've chosen to let life be easy, to align with your purpose, and to embrace your unique essence. Now, you seal that choice with love, with commitment, and with the unwavering belief that ease gets to be yours. Stand in your power. Claim it. Don't just be the hero; be a damn dragon.

CHAPTER 10

DO YOU GROK IT?

"When you give someone your manual, you teach them how to love you."

—Julia Henning

"I am not afraid. I was born to do this."

—Paraphrase of a statement attributed to Joan of Arc (because the original had a lot more about soldiers, God, and noblemen—this version gets right to the point)

EMBRACING THE EASE YOU'VE EARNED

Oh yeah, I'm quoting myself, baby! Because before you can hand over that manual to someone else, you've got to know it inside and out yourself. And that's where this chapter comes in—making sure you've got your own manual down to the point where it's second nature. It's like knowing your recipe so well that you can whip it up anywhere and anytime.

But before we bind that manual of life lessons, we have to make sure you grok it. Yes, *grok*. I first heard that word in my Eastern Philosophies class back in college. Out of all the pearls of wisdom we explored, this one stuck with me like nothing else. To grok something isn't just to understand it in the intellectual sense—it's to absorb it, to let it seep into your very being. It's a knowing that transcends mere comprehension, sinking deep into your bones, your heart, and your soul. It's as if the concept becomes part of your DNA, shaping the way you move through the world. When you truly grok something, it's no longer just knowledge—it's lived experience, instinctual and effortless. It was the first lesson the professor provided us, and I grokked why. If we couldn't deeply internalize the philosophy, it had little chance of actually shifting our perspective.

The word itself comes from Robert Heinlein's sci-fi novel *Stranger in a Strange Land,* and it's all about that deep, intuitive understanding that feels like it's part of your very being. My philosophy professor loved to throw it out there as a challenge: *Do you grok it?* And at first, I'll admit, it sounded like something from a sci-fi convention. But the more we explored the concept, the more I realized it was pure gold. Grokking isn't just about getting it—it's about *living* it. Over the years, *grok* has become a staple in my vocabulary, even if it does get me some side-eye now and then. But here's the thing: once people hear it, they start using it too. There's something about the concept that resonates on a deep level. It's like a shortcut to real, embodied understanding, and once you grok something, it sticks with you for life.

So as we wrap up this journey, I want to make sure you're not just passively reading—you're grokking. This chapter is about making sure all the wisdom we've unpacked together isn't just floating around in your head like a bunch of loose ideas but has fully integrated into your life, becoming a part of your manual.

This chapter is the crucial stitch that pulls the whole tapestry together, the point where everything we've explored finally locks into place. It's about ensuring that these concepts aren't just things you've learned—they're now part of how you live, breathe, and navigate the world. Let's not sugarcoat it: life doesn't just become effortlessly easy because you've decided to embrace ease. It takes consistent effort, daily choices, and a commitment to your well-being. But here's the beautiful part: the more you choose ease, the more it becomes a natural state of being. The end of this book is the start of a new chapter in your life, one that's filled with possibility, authenticity, and ease.

So, do you really grok it? Do you grasp, in the deepest part of you, that life doesn't have to be a constant struggle? That ease isn't about avoiding challenges but embracing your true self in a way that makes everything flow more naturally? Do you understand that you've crafted a manual, not just for others to learn how to love you, but for yourself—to live authentically, to embrace ease, and to find joy in being exactly who you are?

Throughout these pages, you've been on a journey of discovery. You've explored your values, your desires, your true essence. You've navigated the complexities of relationships, the necessity of setting boundaries, and the power of authenticity. You've learned to listen to yourself, to honor your truth, and to let go of the things that don't serve you. You've expanded your window of tolerance, made space for growth, and embraced the ripples of change.

But now, it's time to take all of that and truly live it. In this chapter, I won't add new tools or fresh insights. Instead, I want to give you a chance to step back and realize that you already have everything you need. It's about embodying the wisdom you've gained and letting it guide you through every moment of your life.

HARD-WON LESSONS

This book was conceived from the life lessons I wish I had been taught, as opposed to the platitudes I was raised on. Growing up, my dad's platitudes and my perception of my family's limited capacity for emotional conversations were a constant source of tension for me. It drove me crazy, those one-liners that seemed to oversimplify the complexities of life. I wanted more. I wanted those after-school, heart-to-heart talks when parents lay out the facts of life, arming their kids with tips, tricks, and tools to navigate its complexities—or when siblings teach you the ways of the big, wide world. In my experience, these moments always felt just out of reach—idealistic, maybe even a little unrealistic.

This book is a compilation of the insights I gained by choosing the hard paths, by touching the fire, and by daring to discover, test, and validate who I truly am. But while some might receive the life lessons that feel like answers in the void early on in life, I don't regret my upbringing or the choices I made. Those experiences led me here—to this moment, to this book, and ultimately, to you. (And I can now solidly say that my commitment to myself has not only healed my desire for deeper fulfillment but also profoundly rippled into my family, allowing us to share our feelings and authenticity with ease. I even ask for a platitude from time to time.)

I've been known as the patron saint of burnout and overreaction, making things harder on myself than they needed to be. But through all that, I slowly evolved into something more—a goddess of expression, a beacon of authenticity, and a living, breathing permission slip to remind you that life can be easy if you let it. Sure, no one has it easy all the time, but ease is something we can seek out, something we can cultivate once we understand what it truly means for each of us.

I'm grateful for my life lessons, for my upbringing, and for my parents and what they taught me. And one day, I hope to pass on these lessons to my own child, to sit them down and share the wisdom I've gained. (Fair warning: there's another book, or love letter, on the way). But when it came time to finish this book, instead of compiling a cheat sheet of what you've learned, I realized I just wanted to remind you that life gets to be easy if you let it.

In this book, you've created your manual, mostly by reading mine. And while some might challenge me with concepts like attachment styles, love languages, and the idea that people do things differently (I hear you—I am a psych master, after all), at the end of the day, this book was written to answer a question I've been asking since childhood: What is the point? Specifically, what is the point of being human? Of being me? Of being you? (No, really. Other kids were zoning out in the backseat of the minivan, and I was asking, "Mom, who is Julia?!" Imagine the shock of a five-year-old earnestly asking this from the rearview mirror.)

We all agree that life is tough, but isn't the point of it all love? Isn't that what we're all yearning for, seeking, fighting for, and surrendering to over and over again? Even when we're pursuing more money, expanding social circles, or seeking fame, the deepest motivation is to find happiness, joy, and fulfillment—all just different flavors of love. And doesn't love feel like ease when it's true? In writing this book, I wanted to give you the manual I wish I'd had—a guide not just for surviving but for thriving. A manual to loving life and letting it be easy.

I didn't claim to know it all or promise perfect results, but I'll be damned if you didn't learn something, reconsider something, or change something after reading this. And if, after finishing, you're thinking, *My god, this woman somehow wrote a book about self-development by talking about recipes, compasses, and Taylor Swift,* I'd say you're damn right. Because I let it be easy. Because I'm a master of my authenticity. And you, my dear, can be too.

One day, I asked my dad—out of the blue and with little context—what ease meant to him. His response, which I'll now share with you, is a reminder that there isn't a perfect definition or a one-size-fits-all answer. But through these principles and lessons, a happy, successful, fulfilling, and love-filled life can be achieved—even if the wisdom comes from the most unexpected places. His words weren't perfect, but they were real. They reminded me that ease isn't something you find outside of yourself—it's something you cultivate from within. I told you: it's an inside-out process!

To: Julia Henning
Date: Wed, Jun 26, 2024 at 11:31 AM
Subject: Life ain't always easy.

Hey Sweetheart,

You tell me that sometimes life seems hard…

When you think about it, I guess it's not really surprising life can be challenging when you consider how far and wide life really is. We play so many roles…Father, daughter, friend, associate, acquaintance, protagonist, antagonist, employee, and on and on and on. There are distinct phases in life from infancy through childhood, into our teens, adulthood, and finally, old age. So yeah, sometimes in our lives, things will feel hard to handle. As I look back on my life, I think I've been blessed to have had few truly difficult burdens to bear. Many things have come relatively easy to me. I have always been able to learn new information and develop reasonable skills throughout my life. Looking back, I attribute much of that to the fact that my core beliefs, while they've evolved over time, have remained relatively constant throughout. I was raised with a generally Christian view of the world and have always believed in things like the golden rule and the need for introspection. I'm often labeled "The luckiest guy in the world…" and to be sure, I have had my share of good fortune. But the confidence I've developed over the years by 'showing up' and giving my best effort has given me the strength to take chances that have, more often than not, served me well.

When life does feel hard to me, I generally find solace in the fact that "This too shall pass…"

I recognize that all of life is a play of sorts, and I choose to strive to write mine as a romantic comedy instead of a tragedy. I take responsibility for my failings and move on, trying not to drag others down into my difficulties.

Things seem easy and I seem to navigate life with ease when I'm true to myself and my emotions. It dawned on me a long time ago that I can get incredibly emotionally moved reading a touching story or watching an inspired performance. I strive to be the guy I admire in those scenes because

I know those emotions come from my heart and soul and strike me as universally important.

And so, Zip, I ramble on about how I try to set my course and react to this world. Sometimes, it can be hard, but building an honest life with some humility, generosity, and kindness helps to ease the strain. Most importantly, finding love with your mom, Sarah, David, and always YOU makes life seem easy to me. Thanks for that.

Love always,

Your Dad.

I want you to remember that you have everything you need to live a life that's true, fulfilling, and yes, easy. You've created your manual, and while it may not look like anyone else's, it's yours. And that's exactly as it should be.

This book is my love letter to you, a reminder that you were born to do this—born to live fully, authentically, and with ease. So, as you move forward, remember: life gets to be easy, if you let it. Don't skip that lesson again. Do you grok it?

ACKNOWLEDGMENTS

To the team at Reflek Publishing—Jake, Mikey, and everyone at BIB—thank you for turning my vision-board dream into a reality. You have created a safe space where artists and writers can thrive, and you made this process not only easy but fun. Thank you for believing in this book and helping me put it into the world with such care. Each of you brought insight, wisdom, and unwavering support, and for that, I'm forever grateful. To the team behind the stunning cover—thank you for translating my heart into art. You breathed color and life into these pages and gave me a cover that made me gasp with joy. To Teresa, thank you for your time and meticulous care in editing these pages. You got my voice, my tone, and my humor, and somehow resisted the urge to judge my terrible grammar (thank you for that!). You turned chaos into clarity with grace.

To Anastasia, I couldn't have done this without you. As my writing coach and now friend, you were my anchor on the tough days—when I doubted myself, didn't know where to start, or let the voices of others drown out my own. You were my personal clarity compass on this journey, keeping me grounded in the idea of ease and always bringing your brutally honest wisdom, which few can offer. I am endlessly grateful for your belief in me and excited for the collaborations to come.

To my family, you are my foundation—the most supportive, loving, and united family I could ever hope for. It took us time to find our ease, but now, everything is flowing as it should. Sarah and David, you paved the way, creating paths I now walk with confidence. Olivia and Gigi, you made me an aunt and someone who cared to put good things into the world, let it be easy my loves. Mom and Dad, you made life easy for me, so naturally, I rebelled and made it harder for myself—but your love, acceptance, and unwavering support of my happiness and truth have been the greatest gifts. I am proud to be a part of you and to carry your love with me.

You didn't just tell me about the world; you showed it to me. I love you, and this is for you. Platitudes and all. To Violet, if and when I get to meet you, just know this is all for you. Thank you baby.

To my tribe, my sisters, my covens, and my dearest friends—you know who you are. Through our adventures, I've learned the lessons that fill these pages. You give me ease with the space you hold for me to be my favorite self. I love you all deeply. Special thanks to the sisters who carried me through the writing process: Meredith, Sara, Claire, Alisha, Julia, Celia, Mary-Grace, Stefanie, Dayana, Lindsay, Cindy, Morgan, Meghan, Shanna, Lauren, Jessica, Maria, Laurie, Marie, Tessi, Lily, Shay, Kelly, Jules, Rawan, Chelsea, Miranda, Diane, Mel, Taylor, Priscilla, Tina, Mila, Irina, Vika, Apryl, and Jordana- what started as a conversation in a bar sparked a connection that made this book real. Thank you all for being forces of inspiration, power, authenticity, and love. I am not me without all of you.

To the noble men of my life, you've been rocks and anchors in the deep moments reminding me who I was when I started this venture and who I am becoming as I finish it. You are the kings of the Queendom and the arms that held me in the in between and who are there when you just need to bro out sometimes: Vincent for helping me start this book, Joey, Dr. Carpenter, Nic, David, Brendan, Roscoe, Fred, Ryan O., Ryan T., Danny M., Danny G., Bradley, Chris, Jordan, Brandon, Greg, Matija, Jeffrey, Rudy, Bert, Gary, Garit, Eric, Leo, Ruslan, Evgeniy, and Nikita for helping me finish this book.

To my clients and collaborators, you give me purpose. Without you, there wouldn't be a reason to express these truths. You inspire me to grow and expand, and you bring joy into my life. I am so proud of you and deeply honored to walk this path with you.

To my followers and community, thank you for joining me in the creation of this book. From voting on covers to sharing in my daily thoughts and feelings, you gave me the strength and motivation to see this through. You held space for my process, and for that, I'm eternally grateful.

To the readers, this book is for you and me. It's a reminder and a permission slip to live the life you want and to see being alive as a gift, a miracle, a blessing. Don't block your blessings. You are the ultimate blessing to me, and I thank you for investing in this journey and making it all worthwhile.

And lastly, I thank myself. We should all do this more. I thank myself for believing this was possible, for showing up to do the work, for forging ahead when I felt lost or like a fraud, and for putting myself out there for the world to see. I thank myself for knowing this mattered and for doing what I said I would do. I hope the same for you. Thank you for reading, for investing in yourself as I have done here. May this chapter of your life be filled with ease, as this chapter of mine has proven to be.

Made in the USA
Las Vegas, NV
03 December 2024

13309975R00156